IMAGES
of America

PROVIDENCE
POLICE DEPARTMENT

IMAGES
of America

PROVIDENCE
POLICE DEPARTMENT

Paul Campbell, John Glancy,
and George Pearson

ARCADIA
PUBLISHING

Published by Arcadia Publishing
Charleston, South Carolina

Printed in the United States of America

Library of Congress Control Number: 2014930609

For all general information, please contact Arcadia Publishing:
Telephone 843-853-2070
Fax 843-853-0044
E-mail sales@arcadiapublishing.com
For customer service and orders:
Toll-Free 1-888-313-2665

Visit us on the Internet at www.arcadiapublishing.com

CONTENTS

FOREWORD

The city of Providence is the capital of Rhode Island and the third-largest city in New England. One of the oldest cities in the United States, it is rich in culture and tradition and has a long history of independence and religious liberty. On August 12, 1864, Mayor Thomas A. Doyle signed an Ordinance in Relation to Police that gave birth to the Providence Police Department (PPD). From its humble beginnings of only a handful of night watchmen, today the department has over 400 sworn police officers who proudly wear a Providence Police badge and work closely with the city's neighborhoods to reduce crime, fear, and disorder. The officers are assisted by over 100 dedicated civilian support staff who are critical to the department's mission of protecting and serving the citizens of Providence.

The Providence Police Department's motto, *Semper Vigilans*, in Latin means "always vigilant" and is significant because the department built its reputation on always watching and safeguarding the citizens of Providence and protecting life, liberty, and property. The department gains its authority from the people it serves and enjoys the support of the community because of the professional relationship, partnerships, and trust it has built over the past 150 years. Throughout its history, the department has set a high standard of integrity, respect, honor, dedication, and courage for those who have served and presently serve as Providence police officers.

The department has a long history of success from its early days of serving as night watchmen and its later days tackling the illegal possession of alcohol during Prohibition, dismantling La Cosa Nostra, combating American organized crime, and arresting internationally known gang members rooted in Providence who preyed upon innocent people. The department is always vigilant in fighting the illegal narcotic-distribution business, which continues to threaten the nation. The Providence Police have faced all types of public-safety challenges and adversities and have weathered them all with perseverance, determination, resiliency, and creative policing strategies and tactics. In many cases, the department has received national recognition for its efforts. This impressive record of accomplishment is a tribute to the men and women who proudly wear a Providence Police badge. The respect and reputation of the Providence Police Department comes from the men and women who served and continue to serve, particularly the 10 police officers who made the ultimate sacrifice in protecting this great city. As our brothers and sisters have done before us, every Providence police officer serves with courage, honesty, dedication, and sacrifice to make the city of Providence a safer place to live, work, and visit.

Please join us in celebrating the 150-year anniversary of the Providence Police Department.

—Steven Pare
Providence Police Commissioner

ACKNOWLEDGMENTS

This book relied on the generosity and expertise of a number of people who worked closely with us during its production. Providence City Archives staff members Caleb T. Horton, Nathan Lavigne, and Britni Gorman assisted with research, photograph scanning, and many other tasks. Professors Frances Leazes, Scott Molloy, and Robert Cvornyek and historians Robert Hayman and Russ DeSimone provided both visual images and their expertise. Local library and research centers also offered a great deal of assistance to us. We wish to thank the staff at the John Hay Library at Brown University, the Rhode Island Historical Society, Ken Carlson at the Rhode Island State Archives, and particularly Kate Wells, Rhode Island Collections librarian at the Providence Public Library, for their collective cooperation. Our statewide newspaper, the *Providence Journal*, houses a treasure trove of early photographs, and the quality of this book was greatly enhanced by access to this library, which is under the direction of Michael Delaney. Peter Campbell offered his talents as an artist in creating the image of the night watchman that appears in chapter one.

The Providence City Archives and Providence Police Department archive provided the bulk of primary source materials for this book. We also benefitted from earlier printed works on the department, including Henry Mann's *Our Police* (1889); *Providence and Her Protectors* (1908), published by the Providence Police Association; and Leo Trambukis's *Brief History of the Providence Police Department* (1964). Finally, we wish to acknowledge the assistance of the Providence Police Department, including Chief Hugh Clements, Maj. Thomas Verdi, Sgt. Kenneth Vinacco, Det. James Clift, officers Ronald Pino and Michelle Rudolph, and retired officer Jack Costa.

INTRODUCTION

The history of the Providence Police Department dates back to the appointment of the first town sergeant in 1651. The first Providence Police badge was issued in 1848, and in 1851, "Day Men" patrolled the city's neighborhoods. The following pages highlight the many transformations over the department's distinguished 150-year history, from the city ordinance authorizing its establishment in 1864 to the present day. The department's history is intertwined with that of Rhode Island's capital city. It is the largest and most diverse police force in Rhode Island and is a reflection of the community and the citizens it serves. There have been 38 individuals who have had the privilege of being called the chief of the Providence Police Department, and it is with great pride that I introduce you to the men and women of the department, both past and present. Through hard work and an unwavering commitment to serve, "Providence's Finest" have transformed the department into a nationally recognized police force that relies on strong community partnerships, the latest in technology, and cutting-edge crime-fighting strategies.

Throughout the department's history, those who served and those who presently wear a Providence Police badge have been recognized as leaders in the police profession. The department has introduced many trendsetting initiatives and was the first police agency in New England to establish a bureau of public relations, form a canine unit, and deploy social-service clinicians to serve with officers while on patrol. In 1952, the Providence Fraternal Order of Police (FOP) Lodge No. 3 was chartered and authorized. The Providence FOP proudly hosted the National FOP conference in 1977 and again in 2003.

Over a decade ago, the Providence Police decentralized operations and embraced the community-policing philosophy. We now play a vital role in the community by patrolling from neighborhood substations, attending community meetings, and serving on neighborhood boards and committees. Today, community policing is as strong as ever in Providence, and the results are unprecedented reductions in crime and strong neighborhood collaborations.

From the early watchmen to the specialized units of today, the people of this great city have always relied on the Providence Police as the protectors of their quality of life. Officers who have gone before and those who serve today have all dedicated their lives to serve and protect this community. From the gallant efforts of policeman William Pullen, the first Providence police officer killed in the line of duty, to the valiant and courageous officers who now patrol the city's streets, those who wear the badge remain ready to risk their lives to keep the city and its citizens safe.

Through the years and in response to an ever-changing world, the Providence Police Department has maintained its place among America's top city law-enforcement agencies. The department today is a highly specialized organization prepared to respond to any situation that may arise, and it remains true to its roots of reducing crime and building strong and effective community partnerships. As we celebrate through words and images our 150-year anniversary, please join us as we pay tribute to the men and women who have served and to those who hold our future.

—Col. Hugh Clements
Chief of Police

One

EARLY POLICING

1651–1864

Settled in 1636, Providence became a refuge for freethinkers and religious zealots who had fled persecution in neighboring colonies. In the early years, the lack of laws and structured government threatened the existence of the tiny colony. The first attempt to ensure public safety and protect property occurred in 1640 when the town appointed five "disposers." These volunteers, who committed to three-month terms, were to assist in the apprehension of lawbreakers; however, utilizing volunteers was found to be impractical. Hugh Bewitt was appointed town sergeant in 1651, and he is considered by many to be Providence's first police officer. Bewitt's beat was Towne Street (present-day North and South Main Streets).

War, economic hardship, population growth, and social unrest were important factors in shaping the growth and development of police service in Providence during this early period. A four-man permanent night watch was established in 1775 on the eve of the American Revolution, and as the town's population began accelerated growth, the watch was increased to 12 in 1796. Paid $1 per day, patrolling in pairs, and carrying six-foot-long staffs topped with a hook, watchmen made their way along the town's dark streets, carrying out their mission to ensure that buildings were secure, quell rowdy behavior, or alert the citizenry in the event of fire. Their midnight refrain of "all's well" offered reassurance that peace was being upheld.

By the 1830s, challenges created by population growth, industrialization, and immigration sparked social unrest, culminating in the Snowtown Riot of 1831. A report issued in the riots' aftermath cited lack of centralized control of the watch and led to the appointment of Henry G. Mumford as city marshal. By 1850, Providence was a city of more than 41,000, and a crime wave late that year prompted the city council to establish a 10-man day patrol to supplement the night watch. Thomas A. Doyle, a dynamic visionary, was elected mayor in June 1864 and immediately moved to consolidate the two separate watches under one unified command controlled by the mayor and the board of aldermen. The ordinance creating the Providence Police Department was passed on August 12, 1864, and the department became operational a month later on September 30.

Night Watchman

During the 17th and early 18th centuries, Providence was a small village with a single town sergeant to enforce laws. Sometime around 1698, a town jail was built, but it was destroyed by fire not long after. Pictured here around 1870 is the second town jail, constructed in 1705 on the west side of Benefit Street near Halsey Street. It was abandoned in 1733 after a larger jail was built on North Main Street near Meeting Street, then called Gaol Lane. (Courtesy of Providence Public Library.)

By the outbreak of the Revolutionary War, the town's population had swelled to more than 4,000, making law enforcement increasingly difficult. In 1775, the town voted to establish a night watch consisting of four volunteers who walked the town streets at night in pairs. They had no uniforms but typically carried a six-foot-long staff topped with a hook and a lantern. The night watch was discontinued after the war. (Drawing courtesy of Peter Campbell.)

The early code of laws was harsh by present-day standards. Convictions for treason, murder, manslaughter, burglary, witchcraft, robbery, rape, and crimes against nature were subject to the death penalty. Punishment for counterfeiters included standing in the pillory, having both ears cropped and a cheek branded with the letter C, or imprisonment for up to six years. (Courtesy of Rhode Island Historical Society.)

Lesser crimes, such as making a false accusation or habitual cursing or swearing, could lead to confinement in the town's stocks. The courts hoped that public humiliation would act as a deterrent to criminal behavior. The town stocks in Providence were located near the corner of present-day Olney and North Main Streets. (Courtesy of Library of Congress.)

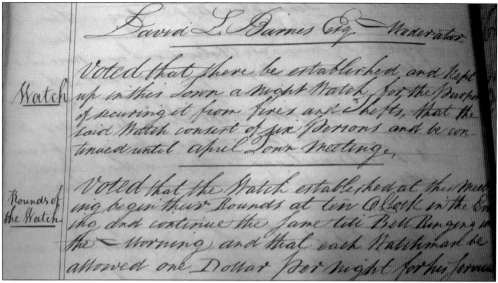

In December 1796, the night watch was reestablished with six men who worked out of a 12-square-foot watchhouse near Market Square. Working in pairs on alternate nights, they patrolled the streets from 10:00 p.m. until "the ringing of the bell" at sunrise. Appointed by the town council and paid $1 per night, the watchmen ensured that all houses and stores were secure, alerted townsfolk in the event of fire, suppressed "riotous behavior," and reported "disorderly houses," according to Providence town meeting records from December 16, 1796. (Courtesy of Providence City Archives.)

Providence in 1800 was divided into three patrol districts. From the central location at the watchhouse at Market Square, one pair of watchmen traveled north along North Main Street to Branch Avenue, a second went south along what is now South Main Street to the Providence River, and a third patrolled west to the Hoyle Square Tavern (shown here in 1875) near the junction of present-day Cranston and Westminster Streets. (Courtesy of Providence City Archives.)

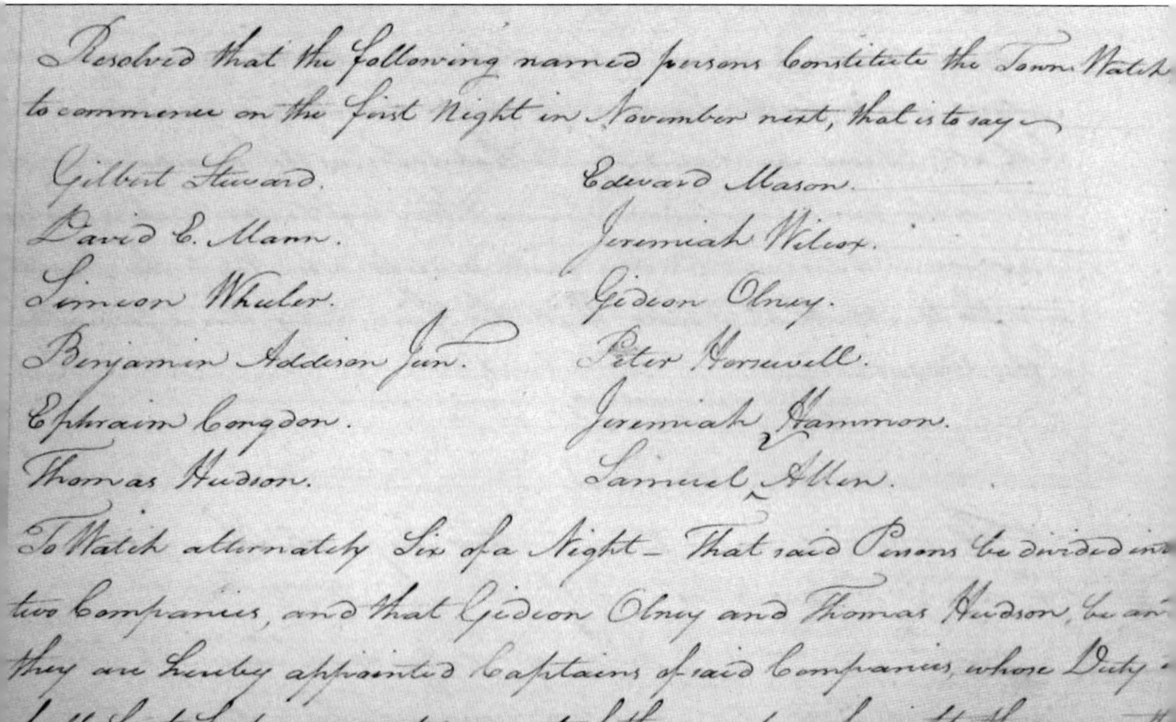

Resolved that the following named persons constitute the Town Watch to commence on the first Night in November next, that is to say—

Gilbert Steward.

David E. Mann.

Simeon Wheeler.

Benjamin Adderson Jun.

Ephraim Congdon.

Thomas Hudson.

Edward Mason.

Jeremiah Wilcox.

Gideon Olney.

Peter Horswell.

Jeremiah Hammon.

Samuel Allen.

To Watch alternately Six of a Night— That said Persons be divided into two Companies, and that Gideon Olney and Thomas Hudson, be and they are hereby appointed Captains of said Companies, whose Duty shall be to keep an exact account of the number of nights they may themselves Watch as also of all those persons who may compose their respective Watch Companies, and that said Captains make report accordingly to the Town Council. Said Watch to be compensated for their Services at and after the rate of One Dollar for each and every Night that they may each of

New regulations adopted by the town council in October 1806 provided for the appointment of 12 watchmen led by a captain. Watchmen were also given authority to jail anyone on town streets after 11:00 p.m. who could not "render a satisfactory account of themselves." Separate rules for blacks included a 10:00 p.m. street curfew and potential jail "if found away from their houses," as well as a late-night ban on assemblages. The council records seen here date from October 28, 1806. (Courtesy of Providence City Archives.)

By 1828, the night watch had increased to 24 men, and the watchhouse was moved that year to the two-and-a-half-story town house (pictured here around 1860) on the corner of Benefit and College Streets. The watch room occupied a 14-by-24-foot room in the south basement. Another 6-by-14-foot room housed three jail cells, each with two bunks. (Courtesy of Providence City Archives.)

SNOWTOWN RIOT 1831

THE SITE OF THE SECOND MAJOR RIOT BETWEEN PROVIDENCE AFRO-AMERICAN RESIDENTS AND WHITE WORKERS

A PROJECT OF THE RHODE ISLAND BLACK HERITAGE SOCIETY

Population growth, immigration, and the influx of sailors into this port city increasingly brought trouble to the string of saloons and dance halls within a black neighborhood along Olney's Lane. A confrontation between blacks and whites on the night of September 21, 1831, culminated in the death of a white seaman shot by a black homeowner. For three successive nights, whites rampaged through the town, destroying black-occupied homes and completely overwhelming police efforts to control the crowds. On Saturday, September 24, Gov. Lemuel Arnold called in five companies of militia, but that night, a large crowd assembled at the corner of Smith and Canal Streets and began pelting the soldiers with stones. The order was given to fire, and four rioters fell dead, with many others wounded. A subsequent report cited the lack of a central command within the night watch as a contributing factor in the tragic rioting. Two years later, Henry G. Mumford was elected the first city marshal. (Courtesy of National Park Service.)

Providence became a chartered city in 1832, but vestiges of the old system of punishment persisted. As late as the mid-1830s, state law still allowed the use of stocks, whipping, the pillory, and the branding iron for 15 separate offenses, including dueling, larceny, and polygamy. The last instance of public whipping was carried out on July 14, 1837, to a convicted horse thief on the green in front of the courthouse (now the Old State House on Benefit Street, seen in this engraving from 1883). The statute was changed a year later to eliminate this vestige of harsh colonial justice. (Courtesy Providence City Archives.)

The Providence City Guards

A confrontation of another kind—the Dorr Rebellion—challenged the authority of the night watch. In June 1842, during the height of the rebellion, a force of 200 "City Guards" (including many black volunteers) took control of the streets, overwhelming the much smaller contingent of watchmen. Dorr supporters in this 1842 broadside depicted the city guards as an unruly band of misfits. Quiet soon returned, and Thomas Wilson Dorr, the "People's Governor" and leader of the rebellion, was sent to the state prison. (Courtesy of Russell DeSimone.)

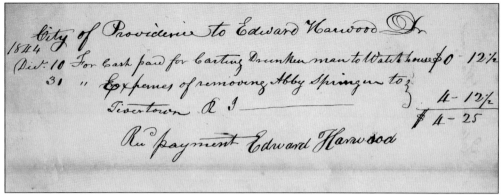

The three jail cells at the watchhouse were frequently filled with rowdies, like a drunken man carted in on December 10, 1844. Lacking patrol wagons, the watchmen relied on city sergeant Edward Harwood to transport lawbreakers to the watchhouse. A room adjacent to the jail cells was reserved for the homeless. By the mid-1840s, the city's population exceeded 30,000—more than double that of 20 years earlier—placing an increasing strain on the resources of the night watch. (Courtesy of Providence City Archives.)

This is the duty ledger of the first watch for June 1844. This watch consisted of 12 men who were paid $1 per night, and their captain, Avery Allen, who received $1.25. Allen was appointed captain in 1832 and served in that post for more than 20 years. The second watch had an equal complement of men. (Courtesy of Providence City Archives.)

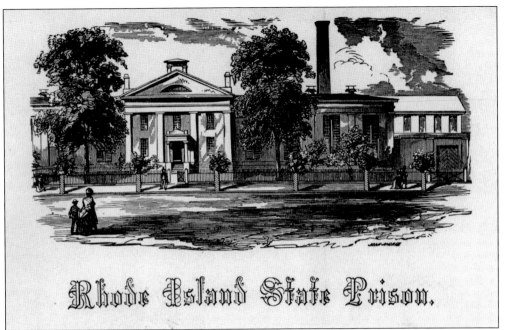

Rhode Island State Prison.

Some of the city's most celebrated lawbreakers found their way to the Rhode Island State Prison. Opened in November 1838 at the west edge of the cove basin (now the site of Providence Place Mall), it listed among its inmates "the People's Governor," Thomas Wilson Dorr, and John Gordon, an Irishman convicted on circumstantial evidence of killing industrialist Amasa Sprague. Gordon was executed in the prison yard in February 1845 and was the last person in Rhode Island to suffer the death penalty. (Courtesy of Rhode Island State Archives.)

Ill-equipped and undermanned, the night watch was hard pressed to provide adequate protection for the rapidly growing city. In December 1850, thieves terrorized the city for several weeks, with one commentator labeling Providence "the best robbed city in the union." Some neighborhoods resorted to hiring private watchmen. The city responded late that month by designating the city marshal, city sergeant, and a new 10-man daytime force of "permanent police officers," providing them with firearms. With the mayor empowered to appoint the night watch and the council the daytime force, patronage was split but the force lacked coordinated authority. (Courtesy of Providence Police Archive.)

The first recorded police fatality in the line of duty occurred on the night of May 18, 1852. At about midnight, 59-year-old William Pullen, a 20-year veteran of the night watch, and his partner went to the aid of another watchman attempting to arrest four rowdy partygoers. A vicious fight ensued in front of the City Hotel, with one club-wielding thug striking Pullen on the head. A second blow hit Pullen's head while he lay prostrate on the ground. He died the following morning. The murderer, later identified as Charles Reynolds, a factory worker at the New England Butt Company on Pearl Street, escaped and allegedly fled to Europe. Pullen's remains were laid to rest at the North Burial Ground. (Courtesy of Francis Leazes Jr.)

The first Providence Police badge was adopted in 1848. Its eight-point–star design was similar to the New York badge issued three years earlier. The Providence badge was made of brass, while the New York badge was fashioned from stamped roofing copper. It is said that the slang word *cop*, or *copper*, derived from the copper badge. Providence night watchmen refused to wear their badges, preferring an inconspicuous coat pocket out of concern for being targeted by bands of ruffians. An 1850 city ordinance required them to wear the shields on their coat lapels. (Courtesy of Providence Police Archive.)

Police equipment included a wooden rattle or clapper that could be used to alert neighbors to a fire threat or help summon other watchmen to assist in making an arrest or quelling a disturbance. Held by its handle and swung, it made a distinctive—and loud—clicking sound. (Courtesy of Providence City Archives.)

By 1860, the police headquarters, housed in a 137-year-old building on Benefit Street, had long outlived its usefulness. Described by the local press as "unfit for a plague hospital," it was torn down that year. The police moved to a temporary headquarters at the Water Witch Engine Company 6 building (pictured) near the corner of Benefit and College Streets. (Courtesy of Rhode Island Historical Society.)

In April 1861, the city police moved to a spacious new three-story brick Central Police Station. Located on the corner of Haymarket and Canal Streets and built on the site of the former jail, it contained 22 cells (one padded), a "tramps quarters" with two rows of wooden bunks, and a morgue. There were rooms for the captains and a library. The second floor housed the 6th District and police courts; and the top level, sleeping apartments for the night force. Homeless staying overnight in the station were required to split wood for two hours at the Charity Wood Yard. In addition to housing, they also received a "substantial" breakfast. (Courtesy of Providence City Archives.)

Providence mayor Thomas A. Doyle is credited with being "the father of the police force." Intelligent and strong-willed, with a clear vision for the city's future, Doyle saw the limitations of a divided, undermanned force in a rapidly growing city of 55,000 people. In his first inaugural address, he called for a complete reorganization of the force "under one head and wearing a common uniform." (Courtesy of Providence City Archives.)

AN ORDINANCE IN AMENDMENT OF AN ORDINANCE ENTITLED

"AN ORDINANCE IN RELATION TO POLICE."

It is ordained by the City Council of the city of Providence as follows

SECTION 1. The permanent Police Officers of the City of
2 Providence shall consist of a City Marshal and *not exceeding* one hundred and
3 three Police Constables, who shall also be City Watchmen, and
4 who shall perform such duties by day and by night, either as
5 police constables or city watchmen, or both, as they may be
6 detailed for by the Mayor of said City; and they shall have all
7 the power and authority that police constables and city watch-
8 men now have by the laws of the State, the Ordinances of the
9 City, and the orders, rules and regulations of the Board of
10 Aldermen; and shall, when on duty, wear such uniform as the
11 Board of Aldermen may direct.

SEC. 2. Said Police Constables shall be appointed by the
2 Mayor of said City, by and with the consent of the Board of
3 Aldermen; and shall hold their offices until vacated by death or
4 resignation, or until they shall be removed therefrom by the
5 Mayor.

SEC. 3. The Mayor, by and with the consent of the Board
2 of Aldermen, shall appoint one of said Police Constables to be
3 Captain of Police, five of them to be Sergeants of Police.

Sec 4. The Mayor may assign any of said Police Constables to act as Detectives, Patrolmen, or Door men in his discretion and shall have power to detail any of the Police

SEC. 5. The Mayor and Aldermen may make, from time to
2 time, such rules and regulations for the government, disposition
3 and management of said Police Constables as they may deem
4 expedient; provided the same are not repugnant to the laws of
5 the State and the Ordinances of the City of Providence.

Approved the same day

Thos A Doyle
Mayor

Acting on the mayor's recommendation, on August 12, 1864, the city council passed an Ordinance in Relation to Police. Following Doyle's wish, the day and night forces were combined and expanded to an authorized force of up to 103 men, with 20 day and 72 night patrolmen led by Thomas W. Hart, the city marshal. Five district stations (on Canal, Mill, Wickenden, Knight, and Richmond Streets) were each staffed by a sergeant. The police force also included superintendents of lights and hacks. All power of appointment was given to the mayor with the consent of the board of aldermen. Providence's modern police force had been born. (Courtesy of Providence City Archives.)

Two

POLICING A GROWING CITY
1865–1918

The city's new 103-man police force, which began patrolling in the fall of 1864, was confronted with a rapidly expanding industrial city whose inhabitants, many from alien lands, were lured to the area by the promise of jobs. During the period between the end of the Civil War and the outbreak of World War I, the city would triple in size, with eight annexations, and its population would more than quadruple. Unlike their predecessors, who had little real power and were essentially a corps of observers, the department's officers were a proactive force, often enforcing the rule of law with clenched fists and nightsticks.

Many Irish, battle hardened by the Civil War, found police work an attractive entry point into the middle class, and by the first decade of the 20th century, Irish had risen to the highest command levels in the department. In the 1870s, the department created a network of six precincts in an effort to raise police visibility and improve response, and by 1916, there were eight district stations in operation along with an impressive Central Station on Fountain Street. New technologies were embraced by the police to improve communication with foot patrolmen and as an aid in criminal investigation. Telephones first made their appearance in 1879, and signal boxes came a short time later. Photography was employed, and the Bertillon body-measurement system was adopted by the PPD in 1903. Detectives Patrick "Paddie" Parker and James Swan gained national prominence for collaring some of the country's most notorious criminals.

The dawn of the 20th century brought the advent of the automobile, and with it came unforeseen challenges in regulating this new technological innovation. The year 1902 saw the first highway fatality, and in 1911, a new set of ordinances governing traffic led to creation of a 19-man traffic squad to help ensure pedestrian safety and direct traffic. By the end of the period, the department too had purchased its first police vehicles, and soon, the four-legged mounted steeds would be replaced by two-wheel motorcycles.

This is a composite photograph of the PPD force in the 1860s. Mayor Thomas Doyle designed the police badge and buttons. Police had to buy their uniforms, but the city purchased the cloth and sold it to them at cost. John T. Brown was said to be the first patrolman to appear on local streets in uniform in April 1865. A local reporter writing for the *Providence Post* described the blue uniforms as "very neat . . . although we cannot say much for the cap." (Courtesy of Providence Pubic Library.)

In 1866, the city marshal post was abolished and replaced by a chief of police. Gen. Nelson Viall became the city's first police chief that year. Genial and well respected, his military career spanned both the Mexican War and the Civil War. In the latter conflict, Viall saw action at Bull Run, Antietam, Fredericksburg, and a number of other engagements, eventually achieving the rank of brevet brigadier general. His term as chief was short. A year after his appointment, General Viall resigned to become warden of the Rhode Island State Prison. (Courtesy of Providence City Archives.)

NELSON VIALL.

Benjamin H. Child enlisted in the Army in June 1861 at the age of 19 and was attached to Battery A, 2nd Rhode Island Artillery Company. Seeing action at a number of battles, he was wounded three times, and for his heroics at the Battle of Antietam, he was awarded the Medal of Honor. Child was appointed a police officer by Mayor Doyle in June 1874 and quickly rose through the ranks, becoming chief in January 1881. He served in that post until 1896. Child died in 1902 at the age of 59. (Courtesy of Providence City Archives.)

Although the department was organized as a professional force in 1864, little financial provision was made for officers injured on the job or those who retired from service. Police heroics during a flood that ravaged the city in 1867 and a fire that year prompted several donations to the department by appreciative businessmen. In March 1870, these funds served as the foundation for the creation of the Providence Police Association, whose operations were administered by a board of directors. Pictured here is the board members from the late 1880s. By 1887, a $1,000 benefit was provided to widows of deceased officers, and $400 was given to officers who had become widowers. A daily sick benefit of $1 was paid to officers after a one-week illness. Efforts to replenish this fund led to the creation of the Policeman's Ball. (Courtesy of Providence City Archives.)

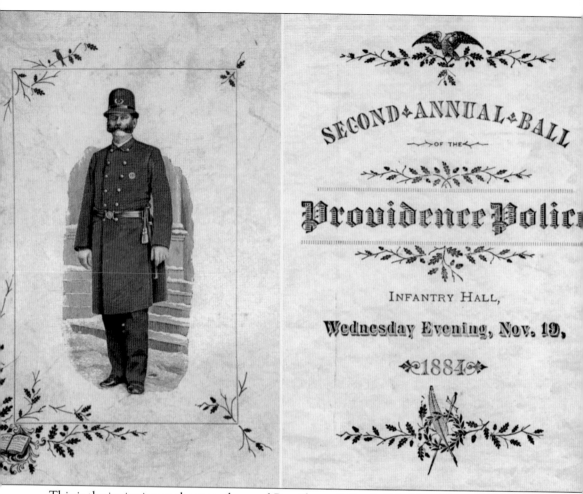

SECOND ANNUAL BALL
OF THE
Providence Police

INFANTRY HALL,
Wednesday Evening, Nov. 19,
1884

This is the invitation to the second annual Providence Police Ball, held on November 19, 1884, at Infantry Hall on South Main Street. The evening featured waltzes by Strauss, Sullivan, and others, performed by D.W. Reeves and his American Band. (Courtesy of John Glancy.)

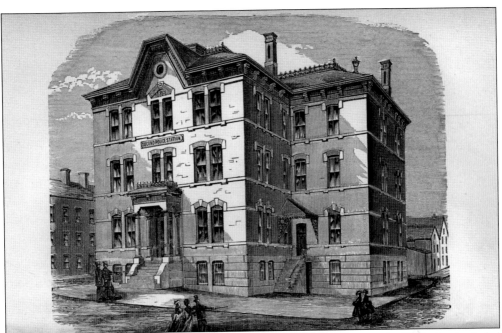

At the urging of Mayor Doyle, a modernization program was carried out in the 1870s that included a reorganization of the police department and the construction of three new district stations along with a new police headquarters. The city was divided into six police precincts. District 1 remained on Canal Street. In 1876, a new brick District 2 station (pictured) opened on the corner of Chalkstone and Ashburton Streets near Randall Square. The three-story brick-and-granite station boasted an armory for drills, offices, a room with 20 holding cells, a library, and 10 sleeping rooms, as well as a smoking and reading room. The third floor contained additional sleeping rooms and a "first-class gym" furnished with citizen donations. (Courtesy of Providence Police Archive.)

In 1875, a large, three-story brick District 3 station was opened on the corner of Wickenden and Traverse Streets in Fox Point. The station was shared with the fire department and housed Hose Company 15 and Hook and Ladder No. 15. It was abandoned in 1952. (Courtesy of Providence Police Archive.)

Also finished in 1875 was the three-story Knight Street (4th District) station. Located in the city's West End between Westminster and Cranston Streets, it replaced an earlier station that was destroyed by fire following a lightning strike. (Courtesy of Providence Police Archive.)

In 1851, a combined police and fire station was constructed on Richmond Street to serve the area south of the downtown. Rapid development on the south side and along its waterfront combined with the annexation in 1868 of a 3.61-square-mile area of Cranston made the construction of a larger station house a priority. Land was secured on the corner of Plain and Borden Streets, and in 1885, a handsome, 70-by-49-foot, three-story structure of Springfield brick with granite trim opened its doors. Considered "the model police station of New England," it featured the latest in modern technology—telephones and speaker tubes—as well as sand-filled walls to muffle sounds and a state-of-the-art ventilation system. Called "the Fighting 5th," its precinct patrolmen faced the daily challenge of controlling tightly packed Irish neighborhoods, seedy waterfront docks, and an overabundance of saloons and gambling houses. Capt. Peter F. Gilmartin (front, right) became chief of the PPD in 1918. The structure survives today as a medical office building. (Courtesy of Providence Police Archive.)

Another six square miles of land containing 2,000 homes and 30 miles of streets was annexed to Providence from North Providence in 1874, and an "unfit" wood-frame police station house on Capron Street was acquired in the process. This new area became District 6, and in 1890, a modern precinct station was constructed on Chaffee Street. Abandoned as a police station in 1947, the building more recently was used as a church but is currently vacant. (Courtesy of Providence Police Archive.)

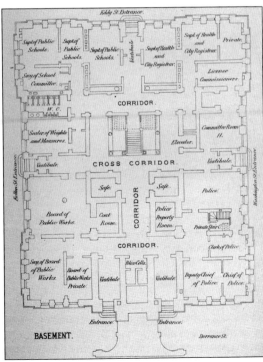

Mayor Doyle's crowning achievement was the construction of an impressive new city hall. Completed in 1878, it provided for the centralization of all city departments, including the police department. The basement (now first floor) included space for the chief and deputy chief, a property room, office space, as well as two holding cells. The former chief's office is now occupied by the city's board of canvassers. (Courtesy of Providence City Archives.)

Patrick Egan epitomized the growing attraction of a career in police work for the Irish as a stepping stone to social acceptance and upward mobility. Like many local Irish, Egan (then 15) joined the 3rd Rhode Island Volunteers just after the outbreak of the Civil War and survived a three-year enlistment. Their service in the war helped mute bigotry against the Irish. In 1868, Mayor Doyle recruited him into the police force. Egan quickly distinguished himself in helping clean up crime-ridden Federal Hill, but he suffered serious injury in the arrest of violent criminal "Pete" Hackett. Egan's exemplary work both in Federal Hill and in the Fox Point district was recognized by the citizens of these neighborhoods, who organized testimonials for Egan that were attended by state officials and the city's elite. Egan rose through the ranks, becoming captain 1876, deputy chief in 1899, and chief of the department on February 28, 1907. He retired in November 1911 after 43 years of service. (Courtesy of Providence City Archives.)

The police department initiated an ambulance service as an "experiment" in 1879. The horse-drawn emergency wagon housed at the District 1 station on Canal Street proved an immediate success. In January 1892, Rhode Island Hospital began its own ambulance service with a wagon supplied by the city. Within a short time, the city supplied two additional wagons for the ambulance service. In 1942, the Providence Fire Department initiated a rescue service. (Courtesy of the *Providence Journal*.)

Also in 1879, a 10-horse mounted patrol was added to the department to monitor the newly acquired suburban areas of the city. The unit proved very effective in protecting residents "from tramps and law breakers who infest the remote portions of the city to beg and commit depredations," according to police chief Charles H. Hunt. Bess, one of the first equine recruits, was said to display "almost human intelligence" in pursuing criminals. First used to give police greater mobility in reaching sparsely populated areas of the city, the mounted patrol became an effective force in crowd control by the early 20th century. (Courtesy of Providence Police Archive.)

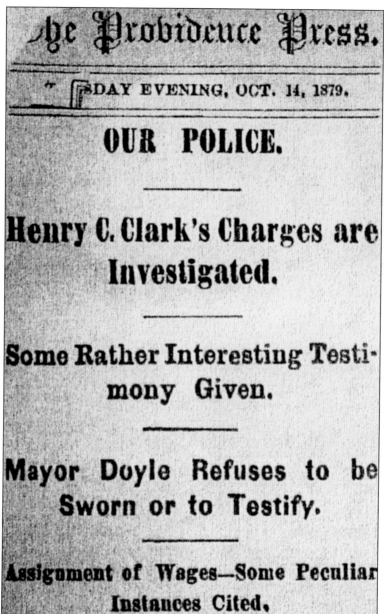

The Providence Press.

DAY EVENING, OCT. 14, 1879,

OUR POLICE.

Henry C. Clark's Charges are Investigated.

Some Rather Interesting Testimony Given.

Mayor Doyle Refuses to be Sworn or to Testify.

Assignment of Wages—Some Peculiar Instances Cited.

In 1879, a major power struggle erupted over the control of the police department. In 1864, all power to hire and fire police, assign details, and oversee nearly every aspect of the department's operation had been vested in the mayor. By the late 1870s, however, there was a growing chorus of criticism regarding Mayor Doyle's "autocratic" control of the department. During one three-week period in 1875, seven patrolmen were fired by Doyle for "negligence of duty and unfaithfulness in patrolling." Complaints, some by former officers, sparked a formal investigation of the department in 1879. The litany of allegations included misuse of the mayor's authority, altering evidence, select enforcement of laws, and intimidation at polling stations. Although many of the charges were never proved, both the city council and board of aldermen voted unanimously (over the mayor's strenuous objection) to transfer the power of appointment of officers from the mayor to the chief of police. (Courtesy of John Hay Library.)

According to Chief Charles H. Hunt, the ideal police officer "should be possessed of a robust and muscular constitution, and of a courageous spirit to successfully compete with roughs and criminals who oftentimes make desperate resistance and fierce assaults upon officers. He should be energetic, temperate and neat in his habits and personal appearance, of gentlemanly address, intelligent and a perfect master of his temper." Police helmets were adopted in Providence by 1886. (Courtesy of Providence Police Archive.)

STAB AND SHOOT.

More Sunday Diversions of the Hot-Headed Italian.

TWO GUISEPPES AT THE HOSPITAL AND ALSO UNDER ARREST.

This Time the Eruption in Little Italy, Tooleville's Rival.

VICTIM NO. 3, THE PEACEMAKER, SHOT IN THE KNEE.

Guiseppe, surnamed Monappeli, and Guiseppe, Surnamed Palmachino, Meet on Sprue street and Exchanged the Time of Day in Italian.—When the Smoke Cleared Away No. 1 Was Found Stabbed and No. 2 Shot, Neither Probably Fatally Wounded.—Another Row Reported on Weeden Street.

During the late 19th century, rapid population growth led by growing numbers of non-English-speaking people created new challenges for police whose resources were often stretched to the limit in an effort to control violence in crowded neighborhoods. This was especially true in Federal Hill, where established Irish often battled with newly arrived Italians for neighborhood dominance. One local paper noted that Italian "fellow citizens . . . night after night seem to delight in cutting up their Celtic foes. We think the old African and Irish feuds will be eclipsed in murderous results by the new Italian war." (Courtesy of Providence Police Archive.)

Providence police, led by "dean of the detectives" James Swan and Patrick "Paddie" Parker, teamed up to arrest some of America's most notorious criminals of the late 19th century. Charles Vanderpool, alias Charles Brockway (pictured here), led a gang of forgers and counterfeiters whose victims—mostly banks—stretched from Chicago to Providence. On August 16, 1880, while attempting to defraud two banks in Providence, he and an accomplice were nabbed in a sting operation led by Detective Parker. Vanderpool spent the next eight years in the Rhode Island State Prison. William "Billy" Ogle was Vanderpool's partner in crime and was arrested with him in Providence. He spent three years in prison but continued in his criminal ways after his release. (Photograph from *1886 Professional Criminals of America*.)

Elizabeth Dillon, alias Bridget Cole (pictured), was one of America's premiere pickpockets. Described as "remarkably tall," the Irish-born thief had been arrested in almost every major city and had done "considerable service" in state prisons and penitentiaries throughout the country. This photograph was taken shortly after her arrest in Providence on February 1, 1879. She spent two years in Rhode Island State Prison. James Dunmunway, said to have been connected to the Jesse James gang, killed 12 men, including a police officer in Cincinnati. His attempted heist of paintings from the Providence Athenaeum was foiled, and he spent the remainder of his life in Rhode Island State Prison, where he killed a fellow inmate. (Both, courtesy of Providence Police Archive.)

PROVIDENCE AND VICINITY,

DUNMUNWAY DEAD.

The Desperate Murderer and Robber Passes Away.

Slayer of Twelve People Dies in a Prison Hospital.

Some Facts and Incidents in a Long Criminal Career.

In September, 1881, a series of daring burglaries was committed in this city, among the robberies being that of the Providence Athenæum, from which institution some valuable pictures were stolen, either by wanton cutting from the frames or by bodily removal.

Perhaps the most celebrated and respected officer to wear the Providence badge was John A. Murray, pictured here in 1879. During his more than half century on the force, Murray left an indelible mark in helping transform the department from a group of untrained night watchmen to a uniformed, organized force of more than 400 men by the time he retired as superintendent of police in 1918. He established a reputation for being incorruptible and good with his fists. Murray was, according to a newspaper account, "the envy of every bluecoat under him." (Courtesy of Providence City Archives.)

Murray's reputation as a bare-knuckle crusader earned him assignments to clean up some of the toughest neighborhoods in the city. Notorious crime spots, like the row of saloons near the corner of Westminster and Union Streets known by locals as "Blood Alley" or the "Binnacle" and a crime-ridden tenement complex on Mathewson Street, fell sway to his rule of law. Murray saw service in the 2nd District, collaring criminals in Chicken-foot Alley off South Main and taking on the "Fighting 5th" District in Irish-dominated South Providence. In one violent episode, Murray was shot in the arm and went to district headquarters, cleaned up the wound, and returned to duty. He later found that the bullet had lodged in his arm. (Courtesy of Providence Police Archive.)

AN INCIDENT OF PATROL DUTY

FIRST OFFICER IN
AMERICA TO LEARN
TRAMP LORE.

Murray may have been Providence's first undercover officer. In 1878, mysterious marks in blue chalk began to appear near homes around the city, causing an element of fear among residents. Murray, disguised as a tramp and living among them on the edge of the city, learned that the marks were a code devised by them. A chalked rectangle near a house meant that the homeowner was kind and generous, an O denoted that the homeowner was hostile, the cross signified a religious household, and a straight line signified a temperance household. An L could mark the presence of a barn or shed that could provide shelter, and an inverted V marked the direction the tramp had taken—with the prongs, not the point, determining the direction. Murray received widespread notoriety for his clever work. (Courtesy of Providence Police Archive.)

Providence patterned its uniforms on Boston's, and during the latter part of the 19th century, police equipment became increasingly standardized. Shown here are Capt. John A. Murray's cap, dark blue winter helmet, .32 caliber Iver Johnson service revolver, ornamental rosewood nightstick with tassel, and, from left to right, wood-handle clapper, come-along, whistle, claw, and handcuffs. (Evelyn Murray Collection, courtesy of Providence City Archives.)

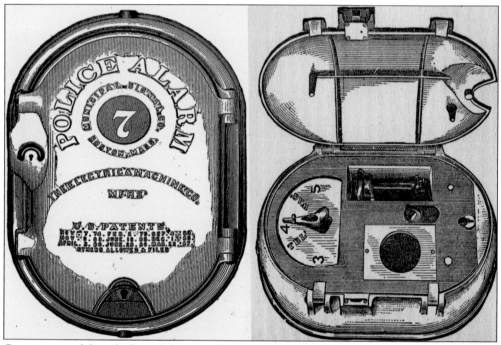

Growing use of the telephone led to another innovation in police communications—the signal box. Developed in the early 1880s by the Gamewell Company and the Municipal Signal Company of Boston, the numbered metal boxes, installed on walls or light poles in patrol districts, allowed officers on the beat to better communicate with their precinct headquarters. During a tour, the officer would be required to turn the pointed dial indicating his route, post, or beat and activate the pull to record his presence. A phone inside the box also allowed for two-way communication between the officer and precinct headquarters. The system, a major advance in eliminating the isolation of the police on patrol, allowed for quicker response to emergencies and enforced greater accountability. (Courtesy of Providence City Archives.)

Lizzie Borden, made famous by her 1893 trial for the murder of her parents, was charged in Providence four years later for allegedly stealing two paintings from the Tilden-Thurber Gallery on Westminster Street. PPD detective Patrick Parker led the investigation, and Chief Reuben Baker asked the 6th District Court for a warrant, but Borden was not charged. (Courtesy of the *Providence Journal*.)

Miss Lizzie Borden.

A warrant for her arrest issued from a local court but has not been served.

Called the "high priestess of anarchy," Emma Goldman had been implicated in the attempted assassination of Henry Clay Frick, an associate of industrialist Andrew Carnegie. Her incendiary speeches drew large crowds and the attention of police, who arrested her a number of times for inciting people to riot. On September 7, 1897, Goldman arrived in Providence and was arrested by police when she attempted to speak at an open-air lecture at Market Square. She was jailed overnight and was ordered by Mayor Edwin McGuinness to leave the city or face jail. Within three months, she was back in Providence, lecturing on the philosophy of anarchism—in Yiddish—without police interference. (Courtesy of Library of Congress.)

Between 1860 and 1890, the city's population nearly tripled. The Central Station on Canal Street was plagued by poor ventilation and overcrowding. In 1893, land was acquired on a block between Fountain and Sabin Streets, and a short time later, a new, three-story Central Station opened for business. The building, a central block with two wings, housed the relocated Central Station, the overseer of the poor, and police court. A basement corridor for a time was used as a firing range. In 1940, police headquarters was moved to a new building a block away at LaSalle Square. For a time, the old station was occupied by the welfare department; it was later demolished. (Courtesy of Providence Police Archive.)

Men of the Central Station are pictured around 1904. Patrolmen were paid $3 per day and had not been given a pay increase in 15 years. In 1899, the force worked more than 155,000 extra hours without pay, and there was no municipal pension. The total police department budget that year was $359,000, and the force had an authorized strength of 300. (Courtesy of Providence Police Archive.)

By 1890, the corrupting influence of politics was becoming an increasing problem within the police department. Political appointments, protected businesses, and rumors of graft led to calls for the creation of an independent civilian police commission to oversee the department's operations, based, no doubt, on successful commission models in Boston and New York. The campaign to establish a police commission began in 1891, and supporters were encouraged by the early success of the Providence Board of Fire Commissioners, which began operations in 1895. The election of William C. Baker, a "Good Government" Democrat, to the mayoralty in 1898 led to the introduction of legislation to create a three-man police commission appointed by the mayor. The Republican-controlled general assembly passed the bill in November 1901 but vested the appointment power in the hands of the governor and the senate. On November 22, former Republican mayor Frank Olney (pictured) was appointed chairman of the Board of Police Commissioners. Despite the controversy, improvements in the efficiency of the department were apparent from the outset. Providence lawmakers were outraged at being politically hijacked and, in 1906, secured "home rule" in appointments. (Courtesy of Providence City Archives.)

Complaints of cramped conditions at the District 7 station on Public Street by Chief Reuben Baker led to the construction of a new station in the Elmwood neighborhood. The three-story brick building on the corner of Potters Avenue and Hamilton Street (pictured) opened in 1902. The old District 7 station was transferred to the Providence Fire Department. (Courtesy of the *Providence Journal*.)

New York police commissioner Theodore Roosevelt established a 29-member bicycle squad in 1895 in an effort to apprehend speeding horse carriages. In August 1905, the Providence Police Department's new 54-man bicycle squad began its patrol of city streets. This was part of the Providence Police Commission's effort to extend the reach of the department to all neighborhoods, improve efficiency, and respond quickly to emergency calls. Officers had to provide their own bicycles, but the city paid for repairs. By 1922, increasing use of police automobiles led to the elimination of the bicycle patrol, but it returned in 1991. (Courtesy of the Providence Public Library.)

Notorious New York gangster Jack Zelig, alias William Golden, was arrested in Providence on August 15, 1912, for attempting to pick the pockets of a passenger on a trolley. He was on the lam from New York City, where he had testified in the grand jury hearing for the murder of gambler "Beansie" Rosenthal. His testimony implicated four killers—"Gyp the Blood," Whitey Lewis, Dago Frank, and Lefty Louie—who were under the direction of corrupt New York Police Department lieutenant Charles E. Becker. Reform district attorney Charles Whitman led a successful prosecution, and all five suspects were found guilty and executed in the electric chair. Zelig, however, never had a chance to testify at the trial. He was assassinated on a Manhattan trolley on October 5, 1912, one day before he was to take the stand. (Both, courtesy of Providence Police Archive.)

BUREAU OF CRIMINAL INVESTIGATION		NO. 1004
POLICE DEPARTMENT	CITY OF PROVIDENCE	

BERTILLON MEASUREMENTS					
HEIGHT 1,76.2	HEAD LENGTH 18.1	L. FOOT 27.4			
OUTER ARMS 1,81.0	HEAD WIDTH 15,9	MID. F. 11.6			
TRUNK 93.3	R. EAR LENGTH 6.6	LIT. F. 9.5			
		FORE A. 47.3			

NAME Wm. Golden,		
ALIAS Jack Zelig"	CRIME Larc. from person	
AGE 28	HEIGHT 5 FT. 9½ IN.	WEIGHT 156	BUILD Med.
HAIR Chest X	EYES Haz,	COMPLEXION Med.	MOUSTACHE
BORN U.S.	OCCUPATION Pick pocket X.	
DATE OF ARREST 8-15-12	OFFICER Henshmarsh	REMARKS:

43

By the 1880s, photography was fast becoming a tool in crime fighting. During the latter part of that decade, the Providence Police Department maintained a "rogues gallery" of photographs of known criminals or suspects displayed in a large wooden case at police headquarters in city hall. In 1885, Alphonse Bertillon, a French police officer, introduced a new system that supplemented photography with a scientific identification system based on physical measurements of the head, fingers, left foot, forearm, and other body parts. Three years later, the system was used for the first time at Joliet Penitentiary in Illinois. (Both, courtesy of Providence City Archives.)

124

The Providence Police Department adopted the Bertillon system in October 1903. The gallery was housed in a large steel case on the third floor of the Central Station within the new Bureau of Criminal Investigation. Pictured here is the Bertillion card for George Eltz, arrested for the murder of his wife's lover in March 1904. The bureau had also installed a new photographic studio, and its files contained more-detailed measurements supplementing the data on the Bertillon cards. Widespread use of fingerprinting eventually made this system obsolete. (Both, courtesy of Providence Police Archive.)

BUREAU OF CRIMINAL INVESTIGATION		NO. 124.
POLICE DEPARTMENT	CITY OF PROVIDENCE	

BERTILLON MEASUREMENTS

HEIGHT 1, 70.5	HEAD LENGTH 19	L. FOOT 27.8
OUTER ARMS 1, 79	HEAD WIDTH 15,9	MID. F. 11.8 +
TRUNK 90.2	R. EAR LENGTH 7.1	LIT. F. 9.4 +
		FORE A. 46.9 +

NAME George F, Eltz.	
ALIAS	CRIME Murder.
AGE 48	HEIGHT 5 FT. 7 IN.	WEIGHT 176	BUILD Med.
HAIR Gray.	EYES Haz.	COMPLEXION Med.	MOUSTACHE
BORN Hartford	OCCUPATION Collector.
DATE OF ARREST 3 26 04.	OFFICER Sergt. Smith #2.

REMARKS: I. Cut tip 2d finger. II. Cute hand scar Y shape.

LIBRARY BUREAU B99958A

Cars first appeared on the streets of Providence in 1900, and within two years, the city had suffered its first traffic fatality. In an effort to control this new mode of transportation, the Rhode Island General Assembly in 1904 passed regulations mandating that automobiles be registered and licensed. Police departments around the country quickly realized the potential of cars to improve their efficiency. Boston purchased its first patrol vehicle in 1903. The motorized patrol wagon pictured here was purchased by the Providence Police Department in 1911 and was equipped with a truck chassis. It patrolled the 5th District in South Providence. (Courtesy of the *Providence Journal*.)

By the first decade of the 20th century, cars, trucks, carts, trolleys, and pedestrians were increasingly competing for space along Providence streets. This photograph shows a jammed Weybosset Street in 1907 during Old Home Week festivities. In 1911, new regulations went into effect to control the use of city streets—designating some as one-way—and a new, 19-member police traffic squad was dispatched to enforce the new rules. The task, according to Mayor Henry Fletcher, was "by no means easy and at times, particularly at first, police authority [was] warmly disputed." Yet, despite the best efforts, accidents and pedestrian fatalities rose at an alarming rate. (Courtesy of Providence City Archives.)

Begun in 1904, the annual October Police Parade was a grand tradition during the early years of the 20th century. Officers and the mounted patrol would often be seen drilling at the Dexter Training Grounds weeks before the parade. Pictured is the mounted patrol passing in review at the Dexter Training Grounds prior to the launch of the parade on October 3, 1913. (Courtesy of the *Providence Journal*.)

Nearly 300 officers participated in the 1913 parade, which made its way from the training field down Westminster Street and through the downtown. The *Providence Journal* reported that, throughout the march, "they were greeted with cheers and waiving handkerchiefs by young and old alike" and that the men "showed the result of past weeks of drilling at the armory." Leading the parade on horseback is superintendent of police John A. Murray. (Courtesy of the *Providence Journal*.)

18 HURT IN RIOT ON FEDERAL HILL; MANY SHOTS FIRED

Immense Mob Fights Police, Who Are Forced to Discharge Revolvers Into Crowd in Resisting Attack With Stones and Other Missiles.

Eighteen persons, mostly Italians, were injured, one probably fatally and three others seriously, as the result of a battle which lasted three hours between the Italians of the Federal Hill district and the police yesterday afternoon.

The affair was the worst riot in the history of the Providence police, and followed closely a battle of Saturday night in which several were injured.

For fear that another uprising will occur to-night the police are in readiness for a battle with the Italians, who have become bitter against the merchants of the district because of the high cost of living.

Several arrests followed the affray and in the Sixth District and Police Courts this morning five men were held on various charges, ranging from reveling to defacing buildings.

The Board of Police Commissioners has taken a close interest in the trouble and is trying to adjust it without any more serious trouble. The board to-day issued an appeal to the residents of the Federal Hill section to refrain from more disturbances, while at the same time they issued an order to Superintendent Murray to use, if necessary, drastic methods to subdue any more rioting.

Councilman V. N. Famiglietti, who represents the district in which the two days fighting has occurred, has appealed

Continued on Page 3, Col. 1.

The growing militancy of labor unions and the increased activity of Socialists, Marxists, and other radical groups presented new challenges for local police departments. The violent 1902 "trolley war" and the 1910 Greystone Mill strikes brought charges by workers, many of them Italians, that the heavy hand of club-wielding police was being used to suppress workers' rights. This simmering resentment helped ignite a two-week, violent confrontation between police and rioters on Federal Hill that left businesses destroyed and dozens injured, some by gunshot wounds. Sparked by charges of price gouging by pasta merchant Frank Ventrone, more than 1,000 protesters overwhelmed a small contingent of police and proceeded down Atwells Avenue on the night of August 29, 1914, smashing windows and heaving the contents of Ventrone's store into the street. (Courtesy of Scott Molloy.)

50

During the pitched battles on August 29, police lieutenant Willis Dow (pictured) exchanged gunfire with an attacker. The following night, police suffered a number of casualties. Patrolman Frank Walters was stabbed, and fellow officer Hugh McShane was shot, possibly by one of several rooftop snipers. Fire lieutenant Robert H. McDonald was shot in the face. Police returned gunfire and made liberal use of their nightsticks. The Labor Day parade on September 7 sparked more violence, but the police had nearly 300 officers ready for trouble, including an enlarged contingent of 23 mounted officers using 15 mounts borrowed from the state armory. Several days later, the "war"—or, as some would label it, "Macaroni Riot"—ended when Ventrone and other retailers agreed to reduce prices of their products. (Courtesy of Providence City Archives.)

The bloody confrontations of 1914 and ongoing labor unrest made evident the need to increase police armament to ensure social order and adherence to the rule of law. In June 1917, the department purchased 100 riot guns and, a short time later, organized an "emergency battalion" made up of Army, Navy, and National Guard veterans split into four companies of 24 men each. Two machine guns were also purchased for added firepower. (Courtesy of the *Providence Journal*.)

Had Your Finger Prints Taken Yet?

First Finger Prints Taken at Police Headquarters for Private Use.

William J. Hershel, an Englishman working in India, is generally credited with developing fingerprinting for court use in 1858. The first recorded use of fingerprinting in a criminal investigation occurred in Argentina in 1892 when police there used a print to identify a murder suspect. By 1901, this form of criminal identification had been adopted by the London Metropolitan Police. The New York Police Department introduced fingerprinting to the United States in 1906, and Providence began using this system the same year. Police chief Murray in April 1914 offered free fingerprinting to Providence residents. Over time, fingerprinting replaced the Bertillon system of criminal identification. (Courtesy of the *Providence Journal*, April 12, 1914.)

By 1915, nearly 230,000 people lived within Providence's borders, and the lower east side of the city saw major residential-construction activity. In response to the growing need for police presence there, the city constructed a three-story brick-faced 8th District headquarters on the northeast corner of Wayland Avenue and Sessions Street. Opened in January 1917, it was staffed by Capt. William S. Kent and a complement of 27 men. (Courtesy of the *Providence Journal*.)

On the night of April 1, 1911, a 25-year-old rookie patrolman named John F. Brennan was working his beat in the Atwells Avenue area when gunshots were heard near Bradford Street. Brennan began chasing the suspects and had apparently grabbed one by the shoulder, but the second suspect approached Brennan and shot him in the head at close range. Fatally wounded, Brennan staggered to the front door of 47 Federal Street and collapsed. He died a few hours later at Rhode Island Hospital. A large contingent of officers was among the mourners that attended his funeral. A huge floral arrangement was sent by the Italian community along Atwells Avenue. Two months later, a well-known local criminal, Bruno Bertucci, was sought in the murder and was wounded in a dramatic gunfight with police. (Courtesy of the *Providence Journal*.)

Providence was a pioneer in incorporating women into the police service. In March 1881, Celia Olney was hired as a police matron. Boston appointed its first matron in 1887, and New York followed in 1891. Generally, matrons were responsible for women and juveniles detained or placed under arrest and jailed at the station houses. Although not listed in the police rule book detailing their duties, by the turn of the century, their mission had expanded to provide clothing, assist with placement in the Sophia Little Home, and offer guidance in helping female arrestees "turn away from evil and accept the shelter and assistance of a Christian home." Evangeline Field, pictured here, is credited with being Providence's first policewoman. A former social worker, Field began her duties as a "protective officer" in November 1918. Given no arrest powers, her work was restricted to patrolling public places frequented by girls and women, investigating missing girls, and assisting police with cases involving females. (Courtesy of Providence Public Library.)

Tue Aug 19th Travelled No 1 Post from 6 PM to 1 AM

Wed Aug 20th Monthly day off

Thu Aug 21th Travelled No 1 Post from 6 PM to 1 AM At 10th PM Arrested William C Prior & Benjamin Flynn on Douglas Ave for Drunkness Assisted by Officer Gillen

Fri Aug 22nd Station day with Officer Cougle. Trav. No 1 Post from 9 AM to 8 AM

Sat Aug 23rd Travelled No 1 Post from 6 PM to 1 AM

Aug 23rd Con.

At 6th PM Arrested Stanislaw Stazok on Charles St for Drunkness with Gillen At 9th PM Arrested John Murphy Joseph McCaughey and John Finn on Charles St. for Drunkness with Sergt Higgins and Officer Gillen At 10th PM Arrested Thomas Pari and Joseph Faloni on Douglas Ave for Drunkness

Sun Aug 24th On watch from 6 PM to 1 AM Travelled No 1 Post from 1 AM to 8 AM

Mon Aug 25th Travelled No 1 Post from 6 PM to 1 AM Telegraph from 1 to 8 AM

This is the duty book of Patrolman James Keegan. Keegan worked out of the 2nd Precinct and regularly patrolled the North End, Randal Square, and Chalkstone Avenue. These entries from August 1913 detail the host of issues confronting patrolmen on the eve of World War I. (Courtesy of Providence Police Archive.)

For the officers and patrolmen of the Central Station (pictured) and their fellow officers in other district stations, the prospect of retirement was not a happy one. The meager monthly pension, funded primarily with court witness fees, extra duty details, and a one percent deduction from police salaries, proved inadequate to provide relative comfort during one's golden years. A major step in providing an adequate pension occurred in 1911 when legislation was passed providing for a pension partly supported by the city. That enactment also included a provision for a single day off a month, which was increased to two days in 1914. (Courtesy of Providence Police Archive.)

Three

PROHIBITION AND THE EMERGENCE OF ORGANIZED CRIME

1919–1930

The growing strength and diversity of the Providence Police Department following World War I mirrored the city's burgeoning multinational population. By the mid-1920s, the PPD reached its historic maximum strength of 539 officers and men, while the city's population reached an all-time high in 1925 of 267,918 residents packed within its 18 square miles. Like the city, the department's ranks during this period became more diverse with the addition of its first Jewish officer, Michael Mushnick, and its first Italian, Umberto Martino.

Controlling traffic along Providence's increasingly congested streets became a major focus of police attention during this period. In 1922, Providence recorded 38 highway fatalities, and during a two-month period in 1923, more than 1,100 traffic accidents snarled city streets. These sober statistics were a call to action. By 1925, the traffic division had been expanded to 45 men, with 11 motorcycle patrolmen chasing down speeders. In 1923, "blue tag" parking tickets made their first appearance, and by the end of the decade, traffic lights were being installed throughout the city. A formal training program for police recruits was initiated with medical exams, physical training, and instruction in city regulations. New officers were required to attend the Police School of Instruction two hours weekly for three years, and rank and file received annual performance evaluations.

The ratification of the Eighteenth Amendment on January 29, 1919, commenced the nation's experiment with Prohibition, which confronted police departments throughout the country with the near-impossible task of enforcement. In Providence, the PPD established a special "Flying Squadron" to combat the illegal trade in liquor, but by the end of the decade, alcohol could be found almost everywhere in the city. Prohibition formally ended in 1933; however, the experiment had spawned organized bands of criminals who had grown wealthy and powerful and who did not hesitate to use violence as a tool to protect their criminal enterprises.

The city's increasingly diverse population created the practical need to have that diversity reflected within the ranks of the police department. Umberto Martino was appointed to the department in April 1917, but service in World War I interrupted his active participation on the force until 1919. Assigned to the 4th District (Federal Hill), Martino's fluency in Italian provided valuable service to the department. The PPD's first Jewish officer, Michael Mushnick (pictured), joined the force in 1926 and rose to the rank of sergeant before retiring in 1946. (Courtesy of Providence Police Archive.)

Peter F. Gilmartin was appointed superintendent of police in February 1918 upon the retirement of John Murray. A 30-year veteran of the force, Gilmartin instituted a police-training program requiring that all police personnel receive formal instruction in general police procedures, state and local regulations, and the latest techniques employed in police work. Recruits were required to be at least 25 years old, not less than five feet, eight inches in height, and 150 pounds or more, and they had to pass written and medical exams. New officers had a one-year probationary period and were required to attend two hours of instruction weekly for three years. (Courtesy of Providence City Archives.)

Police personnel at this time were subject to annual performance evaluations. Descriptors included such terms as "dead one," "thick," "queer," "slow," and "women." Evaluation results could vary widely from year to year. This is the evaluation for John Rogers, who joined the force in 1915 and spent 32 years in the detective division, attaining the rank of captain. He was widely considered "one of the ablest and most popular men in the department." (Both, courtesy of Providence Police Archive.)

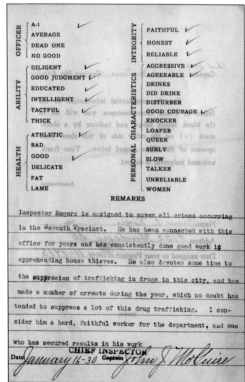

OFFICER			INTEGRITY		
	A-1	✓		FAITHFUL	✓
	AVERAGE			HONEST	✓
	DEAD ONE			RELIABLE	✓
	NO GOOD				
ABILITY	DILIGENT	✓	PERSONAL CHARACTERISTICS	AGGRESSIVE	✓
	GOOD JUDGMENT	✓		AGREEABLE	✓
	EDUCATED	✓		DRINKS	
	INTELLIGENT	✓		DID DRINK	
	TACTFUL	✓		DISTURBER	
	THICK			GOOD COURAGE	✓
				KNOCKER	
HEALTH	ATHLETIC	✓		LOAFER	
	BAD			QUEER	
	GOOD	✓		SURLY	
	DELICATE			SLOW	
	FAT			TALKER	
	LAME			UNRELIABLE	
				WOMEN	

REMARKS

Inspector Rogers is assigned to cover all crimes occurring in the Seventh Precinct. He has been connected with this office for years and has consistently done good work in apprehending house thieves. He also devotes some time to the suppression of trafficking in drugs in this city, and has made a number of arrests during the year, which no doubt has tended to suppress a lot of this drug trafficking. I consider him a hard, faithful worker for the department, and one who has secured results in his work

Date *January 16-30* CHIEF INSPECTOR Captain *John J. McGuire*

In 1925, the city population approached 268,000—the highest in its history—and the city's narrow streets were unable to handle the proliferation of trolleys, trucks, carts, and automobiles. During June and July 1923, Providence recorded more than 1,100 traffic accidents. A year earlier, 38 traffic deaths were recorded, and more than 1,000 people were injured on city roads. By 1925, a 45-man police traffic squad commanded by a sergeant was deployed to help impose order along city streets. The paddles read, "Stop. Always Be Careful." (Courtesy of Providence Public Library.)

Traffic "pulpits" like this one on Fountain Street were manned by police in an effort to control traffic at busy intersections. In 1929, two experimental traffic lights were installed, and by the end of 1930, that number had risen to 55. Local officials boasted that the new signals were "a great leap forward" in controlling traffic. A year earlier, a traffic court had begun operations. The first traffic tickets were simply handwritten notes slipped under the windshield wiper. Later in the decade, so-called See Me Tags were attached to offending car steering wheels. (Courtesy of Providence City Archives.)

The motorcycle squad first traveled city streets in 1911, and its officers spent much of their time chasing speeders. By 1930, the force's 13 cycles supplanted the utility of the mounted patrol, which was retired from service in 1931. The police bicycle patrol was also cast aside by the combustion engine. Both the mounted and bicycle patrols would reappear on city streets a half century later. (Courtesy of Providence Police Archive.)

The Volstead Act, initiating the 13-year era of Prohibition, went into effect on January 20, 1920. Rhode Island, which some called the "wettest state in the nation," opposed the constitutional amendment that made the manufacture, sale, or transportation of alcoholic beverages illegal, and soon Narragansett Bay boasted the largest rum-running fleet on the East Coast. In Providence, the police organized a special unit—the Flying Squadron—in 1925, led by Sgt. Alfred T. Steeves, to enforce the new regulations. This police vehicle was used by the squadron in the so-called liquor crusade. (Courtesy of the *Providence Journal*.)

Unlike Chicago, where 130 gang members were killed between 1926 and 1927, Providence's experience with Prohibition was relatively free of gang violence. During the 1920s, the city averaged about four homicides annually. The war on alcohol, however, was not without its casualties. On the afternoon of February 12, 1928, two police Flying Squadron members—Sgt. William A. Flynn and Patrolman James H. O'Brien—conducted a raid on a house at 9 Booth Street in the city's West End. A quick search discovered two jugs of homemade liquor. When the officers turned to fill out a receipt for the confiscated liquor, the occupant, 22-year old Nathan Brown, pulled out a gun and shot both officers in the back. Both later died at Rhode Island Hospital. The killings were especially senseless as the violation carried a maximum fine of $50, which was usually reduced to $10 on appeal. (Courtesy of Providence Police Archive.)

William A. Flynn

Ingenious methods were used to hide illicit cargo, as exemplified by this car with cases of liquor hidden under the hood. Despite the efforts of the Flying Squadron, speakeasies proliferated throughout the city. Wine was easily available on Federal Hill for $1 a quart, and Marconi's (now Camille's) Roman Garden served booze regularly to Prohibition agents. Another speakeasy not far from the Central Police Station on Fountain Street boasted the longest bar in the state. (Courtesy of Providence Police Archive.)

During the early part of the decade, the police were aggressive in enforcing the liquor laws. In 1925 alone, they conducted more than 2,400 searches, with more than 800 conducted out of the South Side's 5th Precinct alone. This 1924 raid on Gay Street resulted in bootleg booty for the police. The Flying Squadron carried out another 724 search warrants that year. By 1930, however, the growing unpopularity of Prohibition—influenced, no doubt, by the deaths of Officers Flynn and O'Brien and the onset of the Great Depression—led to lax enforcement. That year, only 289 warrants were issued by the department, and 37 by the squadron, which was disbanded in July of that year. America's alcohol-free experiment ended on December 5, 1933, with the passage of the Twenty-first Amendment. (Courtesy of the *Providence Journal*.)

By the 1920s, the old 2nd District station on Ashburton Street was considered beyond repair (the structure had been condemned in 1918), its exterior walls covered with the heavy soot of nearby factories and locomotive smoke. In 1929, the dilapidated structure was replaced by a spacious, new, three-story brick station on Chad Brown Street. Praised by the superintendent as the "last word in architectural design," the building featured a firing range, "waxed battleship" linoleum floors, and paneled light-oak walls. Soon, it would become the home of the police-training academy. (Courtesy of the *Providence Journal*.)

Supt. William F. O'Neill joined the force in March 1890 and spent the early part of his career patrolling the sometimes rowdy downtown streets. Well liked by the local citizenry, he was considered "a terror to evildoers." O'Neill rose through the ranks, becoming superintendent in 1922. During nearly 10 years as chief, he oversaw a department of 539 men—the largest in the department's history—operating out of eight precinct buildings. Despite Prohibition and a city population of nearly 268,000 (the highest in its history), the crime rate remained relatively low. Improvements under his watch included fingerprinting, training programs, expansion of the traffic bureau, and the implementation of a city-supported pension program for officers. (Courtesy of the *Providence Journal*.)

The Jazz Age in Providence produced many great personalities, but none greater than Arthur "Daddy" Black who, during the 1920s, was kingpin of an illegal numbers pool that offered local blacks the long-shot opportunity to win big. A 20-year Navy veteran who was cited twice for bravery during World War I, Daddy Black had investments including sponsorship of black and white professional baseball and basketball teams. His entrepreneurial skills earned him the accolade "Providence's Richest Negro," but his success in the numbers racket earned the attention of a new generation of violent gangsters. On September 24, 1932, Black was shot to death in his office at 160 Cranston Street by a group of black assassins working under the direction of Italian mobsters. An estimated 3,000 mourners attended his funeral. (Both, courtesy of Providence Police Archive.)

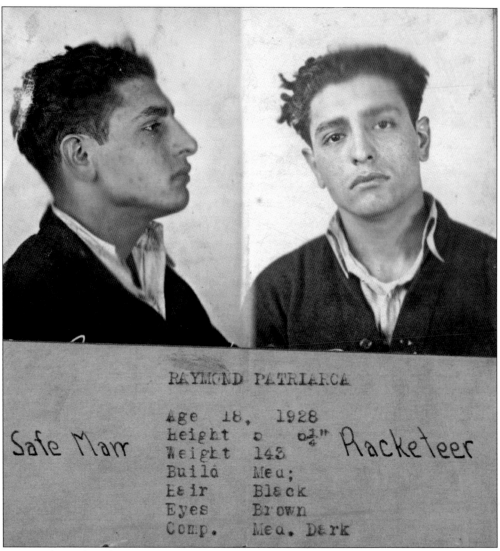

RAYMOND PATRIARCA

Safe Man

Age 18, 1928
Height 5 6¼"
Weight 143
Build Med;
Hair Black
Eyes Brown
Comp. Med. Dark

Racketeer

Raymond Loreda Salvatore Patriarca was born in Worcester, Massachusetts, on March 18, 1908. His family made their way to Providence during World War I, renting a flat at 161 Atwells Avenue on Federal Hill, and by the time Patriarca was a teenager, he had been charged with hijacking, armed robbery, assault, safecracking, and auto theft. This mug shot of the 19-year-old was taken on February 28, 1928, after he was arrested for breaking into Angelo Morocco's store on Pocasset Avenue. His life of crime was only beginning. (Courtesy of Providence Police Archive.)

George W. Cowan was appointed amusement inspector in March 1922. As chief city censorship officer, he was responsible for ensuring "clean, wholesome entertainment" for the citizens of Providence. Following guidance from the National Board of Review of Motion Pictures and the National Legion of Decency, Cowan could ban films or order changes in "dialogue, business, or improper covering" to traveling shows. In his 1929 report, he notes the growing predominance of talking films and the rapid decline of burlesque and vaudeville. At that time, there were 19 theaters in Providence, with a total seating capacity of 20,000. Cowan was city censor for 31 years. (Courtesy of Providence Police Archive.)

What began as an annual parade of Brown University freshmen through downtown streets prior to graduation devolved into a violent riot on the night of May 29, 1929. Students, angry at the "kidnapping" of their freshmen president by sophomores, smashed store windows and streetlamps, lit bonfires, and pelted police and firemen with rocks. Aided by mounted officers, 60 police engaged in a furious battle with rioters at the entrance to the East Side Tunnel. Shots were fired on both sides, and many were injured, including police commissioner Edward J. McCaffrey, who was clubbed to the ground. It was more than two hours before order was restored in the "class war of 1929." (Courtesy of the *Providence Journal*.)

Four

POLICING PROVIDENCE DURING DEPRESSION AND WAR
1931–1945

The police department faced many challenges as the city grappled with the onset of the Great Depression, convulsive political change, a devastating hurricane, and the effects of world war. In 1930, the department's personnel roster had reached an all-time high of 539, but economies forced by the stock market crash of 1929 began to reduce its effective strength. Officers with skills in painting, carpentry, plumbing, and electrical work were relieved of patrol duty to help maintain buildings. The Wickenden Street 3rd Precinct station was merged with Sessions Street, and the 4th Precinct station, on Knight Street, merged with the Potters Avenue station. The city, however, did find the resources to replace the old 2nd Precinct Station on Ashburton Street with a new facility on Chad Brown Street, and in 1940, a new Bureau of Police and Fire headquarters opened at LaSalle Square.

Control of automobile traffic and the consequent spike in traffic injuries and death continued to be a major focus of the department during this period. In 1930, the city experimented with signal lights, and by the end of that year, 55 had been installed along downtown streets. On February 1, 1937, the first parking meter appeared, sparking loud protests from some local store owners. Throughout the 1930s, the police department launched a number of pedestrian-safety initiatives that included the creation of school-safety squads, summer camps, and a major campaign in 1937 that featured billboards and trailers at movie houses, in addition to participation by churches, schools, and newspapers urging the local citizenry to observe traffic rules. The decade-long effort won national recognition and a National Safety Award in 1933.

Politics once again seeped into police operations in 1931 when control of the department was again assumed by a state-appointed commission, resulting in forced resignations and reorganization. Four years later, newly installed Democrats in the general assembly abolished this commission and returned control to a new Bureau of Police and Fire appointed by the mayor. Prohibition had served to incubate the growth of criminal gangs, and widespread opposition to the ban on liquor created a ready market for this new illegal enterprise. The early 1930s saw the elimination of Irish and black gangs and the consolidation of power by a new generation of Italian lawbreakers who did not hesitate to use violence to gain control of horse pools, untaxed liquor, numbers rackets, and other unlawful activities. The growing power of organized crime would become a major challenge for the Providence Police in the post–World War II era.

Democratic control of the city council following the elections of 1928 prompted the Republican-controlled general assembly to abolish the Board of Police Commissioners and replace it with a three-man Board of Public Safety, a state agency controlling both the patronage and policy of the city's police and fire departments. By September 1931, a total of 28 officers had been "retired," many had been reassigned, the detective division was reorganized into squads, and the horse patrol, so useful in the early days of the department, was abolished. Police superintendent William O'Neil joined the retirees and was replaced by James Ahern. (Courtesy of Providence Police Archive.)

Despite the board's stated "policy of economy," it did make investments in new technology and equipment. Horses gave way to these new Chevrolet convertible patrol cars shown here on display near Kinsley Avenue on December 24, 1933. These "mobile patrol" cars were equipped with new one-way radios. (Courtesy of the *Providence Journal*.)

The Detective Division's one antiquated car, often too slow to pursue suspects, was replaced by a small fleet of new, more powerful vehicles. The detectives were also issued new riot guns and submachine guns, popularly known as tommy guns, in an effort to match the increased firepower of local criminals. (Courtesy of the *Providence Journal*.)

A concerted effort by the department's traffic division resulted in a first-prize award from the National Safety Council in 1933 for lowest accident rate among cities of its size. A year earlier, a special school-safety squad had been established to educate schoolchildren on street safety. The results were dramatic. In 1927, there were 55 traffic fatalities on Providence streets. In 1933, there were 21, and a year later, 19. (Courtesy of Providence Police Archive.)

The traffic campaign extended into the neighborhoods, where police on the beat cautioned young bicyclists about the dangers of maneuvering on city streets. (Courtesy of the *Providence Journal*.)

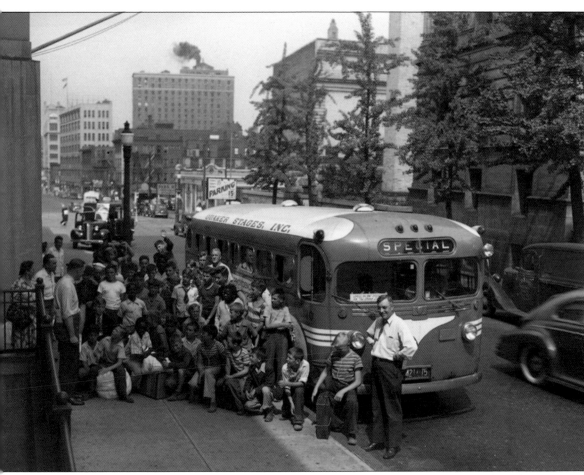

Keeping children off the streets during the summer also helped reduce highway fatalities and injuries as well as juvenile crime. In this July 1944 photograph, Junior Police participants return from a two-week camp. After World War II, Camp Cronin at Point Judith became a popular destination for the summer campers. (Courtesy of Providence Police Archive.)

In the November 1934 elections, the Republicans lost control of the general assembly, and as part of their "Bloodless Revolution," the Democrats abolished the state-controlled Board of Public Safety and replaced it with a three-man Bureau of Police and Fire, with all appointments to that board made by the mayor. On January 1, 1935, Democratic governor Theodore Francis Green appointed state police superintendent (and former Providence police chief) Edward J. Kelly to run the PPD on an interim basis while still retaining his post as head of the state police. The new bureau began operations on June 1, 1935. Joseph Scuncio (above, left) was an early appointment to the new bureau. (Courtesy, Providence Police Archive.)

Retribution was swift. In what was called the "most drastic shakeup in the history of the department," Deputy Chief J.A. Glynn was reduced to lieutenant, captain of detectives Francis S. Barnes was reduced to sergeant, and Capt. James J. Conlon was demoted to lieutenant. Forced retiree James J. Cusick (pictured) was reinstated as chief inspector in charge of detectives. (Courtesy of Providence Police Archive.)

Edward J. Kelly ranks among the most influential officers ever to wear a PPD badge. Born on April 3, 1876, Kelly began his career as a patrolman in June 1900 and, by 1932, had attained the rank of chief. During the Bloodless Revolution of 1934, he replaced then state police superintendent Everette St. John Chaffee, and in early 1935, oversaw both the state police and the PPD. In 1939, Kelly resigned as superintendent to serve as executive secretary of the National Police Chiefs Association, but in July 1941, he was back as state police superintendent. In 1947, Kelly again left that post to become the executive secretary of the International Police Chiefs Association. Kelly was a guest lecturer at the FBI National Police Academy and assisted the FBI in preparing a book on police-training methods. He died on June 18, 1959, at the age of 83. (Courtesy of Providence Police Archive.)

Experimentation with one-way radio communication to patrol cars began in May 1933, and by December, 10 cars had been equipped with radios. This photograph shows radio operator William H. Feeley sending test messages from his radio room at the Chad Brown Station. Patrol officers could receive calls in their cars but had to return calls using outdoor call boxes. Two-way radio communications were tested in the fall of 1935 and had gained widespread use in Providence by 1941. (Courtesy of the *Providence Journal*.)

Major reorganizations within the police department in the 1930s—including involuntary retirements—resulted in many opportunities for those wishing to pursue a career in police service. The city's nearly 25 percent unemployment rate during the early years of the Great Depression also made work attractive. Pictured above are graduates from the 1931 class. The training center on Potters Avenue was later moved to the Chad Brown Station and designated as the Providence Police Academy. A total of 500 applied for the 1936 class, and 92 were successful in completing training. (Both, courtesy of the *Providence Journal*.)

RAYMOND PATRIARCA
Age 33/33, Height 5'6¼" Weight 165 lbs
Medium Built, Black Hair, Brown Eyes
BOOTLEGGER-SAFE MAN-RACKETEER

Named Public Enemy No. 1 by the Providence Board of Public Safety in the 1930s, Raymond Patriarca was briefly interrupted in his criminal career by a five-year prison conviction for robbery. Shortly after he entered the state prison in Cranston, Daniel Coakley, executive councilor to Rhode Island governor Charles F. Hurley, produced a parole petition based on pleas by a Father Fagin, who, it was later learned, did not exist. Coakley was impeached and dismissed, but Patriarca served only a few months. He spent a much longer period of time in a Norfolk, Massachusetts, prison for a 1937 payroll robbery. In May 1944, he was paroled and told authorities he would "tend apple trees in Rhode Island for a living." Within a decade, however, Patriarca was New England's crime boss. (Courtesy of Providence Police Archive.)

The department purchased its first three-wheel motorcycle in 1937 as part of an aggressive campaign to reduce traffic fatalities in the city. In addition to enforcing traffic regulations, the cycles were used in relieving traffic cops on patrol. The relieving officer rode to the post on the vehicle, and the officer being relieved rode the cycle back to the traffic division headquarters. Officers often marked car tires with a chalk line in an effort to nab street-parking violators. (Courtesy of Providence Police Archive.)

Providence police were put to the test on the afternoon of September 21, 1938, when a hurricane with winds in excess of 120 miles per hour slammed into southern New England. At the height of the storm, a tidal surge swept into downtown Providence, flooding areas of the city to a depth of more than seven feet. Patrolmen on duty plunged into the swift-moving waters in a desperate attempt to save those being swept away. Here, a patrolman tries to save the life of a woman crushed by a collapsed building on Friendship Street. The storm claimed 9 victims in Providence and 311 statewide. (Courtesy of the *Providence Journal*.)

In 1938, the city purchased the former LaSalle Academy property on Fountain Street as the proposed site for a new combined police and fire headquarters. That year, the Central Fire Station at the east end of Exchange Place was demolished, and construction on the new, four-story Bureau of Police and Fire building began a year later on the Fountain Street site. In 1940, police vacated their old headquarters, which was later used by the welfare office and other municipal agencies until it was demolished in the late 1960s. In the above 1940 image, police chief John J. Parker (seated, left) and deputy chief James J. Cusick (standing) prepare to leave their cramped quarters for their new headquarters building nearby, shown below. (Both, courtesy of the *Providence Journal*.)

On September 27, 1942, Irene C. Monahan made history by being sworn in as the first female member of the police department. The daughter of George H. Monahan, a captain in the detective bureau from 1915 to 1924, she patrolled the downtown beat "with the powers and duties of a regular policeman," paying particular attention to supervising "numerous 'uniform crazy' teenage girls." She carried a snub-nosed revolver and handcuffs in her pocketbook. Monahan remained on the force for less than three years, resigning her position on September 18, 1945. (Courtesy of Providence Police Archive.)

Lt. James Rogers fires into a wooden ballistics box with a police .38 caliber revolver in this 1940s-era photograph. Fired into the box packed with cotton, the bullet was retrieved and examined for comparison purposes. This box is still in the armorer's room and was still in use until recently. (Courtesy of Providence Police Archive.)

In January 1942, Providence became the first city in the nation to establish an emergency-communications network for air-raid alerts. Avoiding a ban by the Federal Communications Commission preventing all amateur broadcasting, the police department swore in 50 amateur radio operators under the direction of Rev. Charles F. Mahoney (center, standing) as police officers, allowing them to use four radio frequencies reserved for the department. The Providence Mobile Radio Patrol soon established a network of eight stations around the city that were prepared to transmit damage reports to the report center at police headquarters in the event of attack. (Courtesy of the *Providence Journal*.)

Although members of the PPD maintain a sharp appearance in this 1943 parade along Westminster Street, the department ranks had been severely depleted by wartime enlistments and the lure of better-paying jobs in the local defense industry. Between 1942 and 1943, the effective strength of the department fell from 526 officers and men to 429. The $40.25 weekly salary for a patrolman was also likely to include extra duty (for no pay) guarding reservoirs, the shipyard, or the sewage plant. (Courtesy of Providence Police Archive.)

During World War II, many officers were called to serve their country. One was Raymond W. Flynn, a South Providence native, who joined the force in February 1938 and was inducted into the US Army on May 14, 1942. Just over two years later, he participated in the Normandy invasion, and on June 9, 1944—three days after the initial landing—he was killed in action. On May 14, 1950, a memorial was installed in front of the police and fire headquarters in honor of Flynn and another war casualty, firefighter Thomas J. Hinchey. That day, LaSalle Square was renamed Hinchey-Flynn Square. (Both, courtesy of Providence Police Archive.)

Five

RESPONDING TO NEW CHALLENGES

1946–1980

The postwar era presented a new series of challenges for the police department as it coped with the consequences of urban decay, population decline, strained resources, and civil unrest. During 1947, morale among officers was undermined by a major scandal resulting in the dismissal of 13 officers, but heroic crime-fighting efforts by others offset the damage to the department's image. In 1951, the Bureau of Police and Fire was replaced by a single commissioner of public safety, and a top-to-bottom reorganization of the department resulted in the elimination of the precinct system by 1953.

Many factors, both societal and local, resulted in a major rise in the crime rate during this period. Between 1954 and 1964, the robbery, burglary, and larceny rate more than doubled, and auto thefts quadrupled in the city. Major riots in the mid-1960s in America's major cities caused extensive damage and fatalities; in Providence, however, civil-disturbance training by the police and intervention by antipoverty workers aided greatly in preventing large-scale property destruction or injury to the citizenry. During the 1950s and 1960s, organized crime, led by mob boss Raymond Patriarca, maintained a lucrative criminal enterprise, but by the 1970s, aggressive pursuit by city police—partnering with the FBI and utilizing a new crime-fighting tool, the Racketeer Influenced and Corrupt Organizations (RICO) Act—helped crack the power of the mob.

The precinct system enjoyed a brief renaissance in the late 1960s and 1970s, aided by funding from the Comprehensive Employment and Training Act (CETA), but elimination of the program by 1980 led to the closing of the substations. One earlier tradition of the police did return in 1980 when Providence mayor Vincent A. Cianci Jr. championed the rebirth of the police mounted patrol. War veteran Alfred Lima made history in 1946 by being the first black officer appointed to the PPD, and by the mid-1970s, blacks, Asian Americans, and women had been fully integrated into the ranks of the department. The command staff was quick to adopt new technologies in crime fighting during this era and to form tactical units to prevent or respond to new threats to the public's safety and well-being.

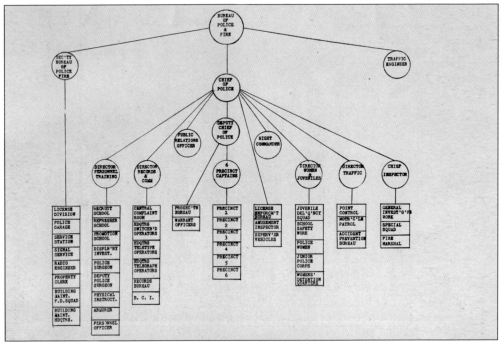

Responding to criticism that the politically appointed Bureau of Police and Fire had assumed almost complete control over the operations of the police department, Mayor Dennis J. Roberts brought in Bruce Smith, a nationally recognized authority on police organization, to make recommendations for improving departmental operations. The resulting—announced on March 28, 1945—and subsequent actions represented the most sweeping reorganization in the department's history. Under the plan, the chief was given sole power to appoint, promote, and transfer personnel. Other changes included reactivation of the Traffic Division, which had been mothballed during the war, creation of a new Division of Personnel and Training, and consolidation of five separate agencies under a new Division of Women and Juveniles. (Courtesy of Providence Police Archive.)

An eventual result of the move to improve efficiency and better manage resources was the dismantling of the precinct system. In 1948, Precincts 3 and 6 were closed, and South Providence's fabled Fighting 5th was converted into a recreation center. The Potters Avenue station (shown here) survived for another five years, but in 1953, all precinct functions were centralized at the LaSalle Square headquarters. (Courtesy of Providence Police Archive.)

Like the Civil War and World War I, World War II provided veterans who were ethnic minorities an opportunity to join the ranks of the police department. In August 1946, Alfred A. Lima earned the distinction of becoming the first black man to join the force. Lima had served more than four years in the Army, more than half that time in the Pacific theater, attaining the rank of sergeant. He joined 40 other war-veteran recruits at the swearing-in ceremony. (Courtesy of the *Providence Journal*.)

In 1948, another new technological advance—the so-called lie detector—was employed as an additional weapon in the war against crime. Invented by Leonarde Keeler, the polygraph was brought to Providence by Lt. Howard A. Franklin of the Bureau of Records after he completed a six-week course to learn how to operate the machine. Franklin at the time asserted that "you can't beat the machine." Here, a PPD secretary agrees to test the new device. (Courtesy of Providence Police Archive.)

One of the most dramatic shoot-outs in Providence Police history occurred during the early morning hours of March 9, 1947, when four officers—Det. Sgt. Walter Stone and Det. Francis Spicola with assistance from Det. Sgt. Charles McElroy and Sgt. Thomas F. McKenna (an expert marksman)—working on a tip, set up a stakeout at the Howard Johnson's restaurant on North Main Street. Just after 3:00 a.m., thieves entered the building and were met by the officers, who ordered them to surrender. One of the three robbers fired two shots into the darkened room. The officers, two with riot guns, opened fire, immediately killing two thieves. The third attempted to escape, breaking through a plate-glass door, but he too was shot dead. It was later learned that the leader of the gang was a career criminal, but his two companions had no police records and were war veterans. (Courtesy of Providence Police Archive.)

The department's first pistol range was a simple sand berm constructed in the 1920s on New York Avenue near Field's Point. In 1933, the firing range was moved to a parcel of land at the old city reservoir in the Sockanosset section of Cranston. It was here that the department's pistol team honed its skills and captured many competitive trophies, including a fifth-place finish in the 1948 national competition, led by expert marksman Lt. Thomas McKenna. Pictured are, from left to right, (first row) an unidentified man and Walter Stone; (second row) Pat Powers, Thomas McKenna, and Clarence Nadeau. This property was sold in 1951, and two years later, a new pistol range opened in Scituate. (Courtesy of the *Providence Journal*.)

Badges were first issued to the night watch in 1845, and following the establishment of the Providence Police Department, a new, round silver, badge with a centered number was introduced. In 1881, another, larger badge bearing the city seal was issued; it remained the department's badge until 1949, when this smaller badge was issued. In 1994, a colored, enameled badge became the standard, with one significant change—the word "patrolman" was replaced by "police officer" in recognition of the growing number of females on the force. (Courtesy of Providence Police Archive.)

The annual communion breakfast was a time-honored tradition for the Roman Catholic members of the police department. Rank and file usually marched from police headquarters at LaSalle Square to the nearby Cathedral of SS Peter and Paul for the Mass preceding the breakfast. (Courtesy of Providence Police Archive.)

During the postwar era, members of the police department volunteered countless hours sponsoring activities for the city's youth. Annual Halloween parties attracted as many as 9,000 children, and the Point Judith Junior Police Camp gave 400 inner-city youth a chance to escape from the hot city. Officers taught model-making skills (below), and police-coached community-league baseball teams (pictured above are the 1949 champions) won several league titles. (Both, courtesy of Providence Police Archive.)

Jeremiah F. Martin epitomized some of the finest qualities displayed by a select group of police officers—personal courage and determination to serve the community despite the dangers inherent in the job. Just after midnight on September 24, 1949, Martin was called to respond to a break-in at Atlas Home Supply at 327 North Main Street. Entering the building, he was confronted by a career criminal who fired at him with a .38 caliber gun. The bullet struck Martin below the right eye, resulting in compound skull fractures and the loss of the eye. Amazingly, Martin, with bullet fragments still lodged in his skull, returned to work in March 1950 and was awarded a medal of honor by the city for his heroism. Despite issues with headaches and nervousness, he continued to perform his duties, retiring from the department on August 5, 1956. (Courtesy of Providence Police Archive.)

One of the most dramatic police apprehensions in PPD history occurred on September 30, 1952, when Louis DiFraia, a 27-year-old who had escaped from mental institutions six times, robbed an East Providence bank at gunpoint and fled through Providence to Pawtucket, chased by more than 150 city and state police and FBI agents. DiFraia was cornered in a house on Laban Street in Pawtucket with two female hostages. There, he fired his high-powered rifle at police, killing Pawtucket patrolman Charles Patenaude. Providence patrolman James E. Cavanaugh was hit in the back by four bullet fragments. DiFraia was wounded in the shoulder, and another bullet grazed his scalp. A *Providence Journal* photographer caught his surrender after the house was teargassed. (Both, courtesy of Providence Police Archive.)

This 1952 photograph of a Providence police car shows the results of the running gun battle with DiFraia. (Courtesy of Providence Police Archive.)

The Fraternal Order of Police (FOP) was founded by two Pittsburgh patrolmen in 1915 to improve working conditions and the general welfare of police officers in that city. Three years later, it became a national organization. It was not until June 16, 1952, that Providence officers established FOP Lodge No. 3, and it was not considered a union until 1963, when the state general assembly granted the FOP bargaining authority and the state's labor-relations board affirmed its legitimacy as a union. Commissioner Francis Lennon, police chief Howard Franklin, and the command staff promptly left the FOP, which became the bargaining unit for the PPD rank and file, inclusive of all ranks captain and below. Pictured here is Francis Spicola (right), the FOP's first president. (Courtesy of Providence Police Archive.)

In 1951, the city hired 25 part-time uniformed, female crossing guards to relieve patrolmen from the task of escorting schoolchildren across busy city intersections. Here, a crossing guard assists children on their way to Blessed Sacrament School on the corner of Regent and Academy Avenues. By the mid-1960s, the crossing guard corps had increased to 94. (Courtesy of Providence Police Archive.)

By the mid-1950s, mob boss Raymond Patriarca had consolidated power as New England's crime boss, ushering in a period of mob violence, some of which occurred on the streets of Federal Hill. One early victim was George "Tiger" Balletto, who was shot in the back six times on the night of August 10, 1955, while drinking an orangeade and vodka at the end of the bar at Bella Napoli Café on 93 Atwells Avenue. Police reported that "Blind Pig" Rossi and a dozen other witnesses of the shooting "had been stricken with total loss of memory." (Courtesy of Providence Police Archive.)

This detective division equipment display at the Cranston Street Armory includes .38 caliber revolvers, a Remington shotgun, and a riot gun with ammunition and grenades. On the left are a comparator microscope, which helped in determining the unique ballistic imprints on bullets, and a camera enlarger (most era plastic negatives were 4 inches by 5 inches). The table on the right contains a microscope and fluorescent light to detect fingerprint powder. These forensic science tools used by the Bureau of Criminal Identification were considered state-of-the-art in the late 1940s. (Courtesy of Providence Police Archive.)

The Providence police have compiled an enviable record in the area of traffic safety. In 1959, the department was given the Walker Safety Award, and a year later, the city went 173 days without a traffic fatality—making its rate lower than those of all US cities of comparable size in that category. Police were a familiar site in the downtown in the late 1950s, guiding Christmas shoppers across busy intersections like Weybosset Street near the Outlet Company Department Store. (Courtesy of Providence Police Archive.)

In April 1960, a K-9 corps was established within the PPD to assist with crowd control, and it became an effective tool for foot patrols at night in curbing criminal activity. Once again, the department played a leading role as the first in New England to make use of trained dogs for police work. Fritz, donated by Mr. and Mrs. William LaSalle of East Providence, was the unit's first recruit. He is shown above with Sgt. John Coyne (left) and officer Ed Malloy. Below, Fritz is making the rounds in December 1960 with Officer Bird. (Both, courtesy of the *Providence Journal*.)

Presidential visits to Providence placed a particular strain on police resources. On November 7, 1960, nearly the entire department was on the job to handle large crowds that filled Exchange Place to hear one of John F. Kennedy's final campaign speeches just a day before voters went to the polls. Kennedy's motorcade traveled along Washington Street on the way to Hillsgrove Airport. To the right are officers Ted Collins and (far right) John Eddy. On September 28, 1964, Pres. Lyndon Johnson visited Providence to mark the 200th anniversary of the founding of Brown University. (Both, courtesy of Providence City Archives.)

This 300-horsepower, four-door 1960 Ford Fairlane cruiser was a quantum leap forward from the days of the horse-drawn wagons and the Black Marias. (Courtesy of Providence Police Archive.)

This patrolwoman models her new hat style in April 1963. Despite the smile, female officers assigned to the juvenile division had to contend with a youth-arrest rate that had spiked 26 percent in the previous two years. Three basic methods were used to process juvenile offenders: reprimand and release, referral to a social service agency, or referral to family court as a last resort. (Courtesy of Providence Police Archive.)

First introduced in 1964 and based on a design created by Public Safety commissioner Francis Lennon, this shoulder patch depicts a raised sword with the Latin phrase *Semper Vigilians*, or "Always Watchful," emblazoned across the sword's blade. This patch has been the standard emblem for the Providence Police Department since its adoption in 1964. Although the colors may have changed over the years with various uniform alterations, the patch remains the enduring visible symbol of the department. (Courtesy of Providence Police Archive.)

Recruits James "Chopper" Connell (kneeling, left) and Edward Malloy wrestle as part of physical training during the 25th police academy in 1964. Both officers would have lengthy careers in the PPD serving in both the detective division and as supervisors in the traffic bureau. Malloy was also in charge of a number of police academies later in his career. (Courtesy of Providence Police Archive.)

Like a scene from a film noir set in the 1960s, PPD detectives discuss investigative strategies in the department's squad room. The line-up stage directly behind them was used to view and interrogate prisoners each morning. Detectives pictured are, from left to right, Jeremiah Murphy, Gulio Fuina, Lt. John Eddy, Donald Kennedy, Ed Carroll, Dave Crook, and Horace Craig. (Courtesy of Providence Police Archive.)

The new police headquarters at 209 Fountain Street housed the radio room on the fourth floor. This 1947 photograph shows calls being dispatched from a sound room. Service calls were received by telephone operators (foreground) and communicated to the dispatcher. (Courtesy of Providence Police Archive.)

By the 1960s, the portable radio had helped to accelerate the demise of the traditional police call box as the basic method of communication between the foot patrolmen, like Frank Hamilton (pictured) and headquarters. (Courtesy of the *Providence Journal*.)

This is a typical roll call in the guardroom at police headquarters on Fountain Street in the early 1960s. Sergeants are in the process of inspecting revolvers, nightsticks, and uniform appearance of the officers as they toe the line. Some officers are footmen who will direct traffic at congested intersections throughout the city. All are wearing white, reflective belts that designate the traffic men of that era. (Courtesy of Providence Police Archive.)

Howard Franklin (center) began his career in 1931 as a Bureau of Criminal Identification detective and rose to the rank of chief, serving in that capacity for much of the 1960s. The Mohican Hotel (later Gemini) was one of three notorious strip clubs operating in the downtown area in the 1960s and 1970s. Strippers there were regularly arrested on prostitution charges, and shootings, assaults, and thefts occurred frequently. Pressure from the city finally closed the Gemini in the 1990s, and the building is now a 57-room, low-income housing development. The site of the Peppermint Lounge on Broadway, a favorite of the mob, is now a parking lot, and the Sportsman's Inn on Fountain Street is taking on a new life as a boutique hotel. (Courtesy of the *Providence Journal*.)

The late 1960s witnessed a violent burst of civil unrest in American cities. Rioting in the Watts area of Los Angeles in August 1965 claimed 34 lives, and two years later, major riots in Detroit, Newark, and other cities resulted in further loss of life and massive property damage. In August 1966, Providence police were called upon to quell rock-throwing gangs in the Willard Avenue area of South Providence, and exactly a year later, another outburst of violence, highlighted by gunfire and house fires, led to the mobilization of 1,000 National Guardsmen and a curfew order imposed by Mayor Joseph Doorley. Firm action by police and the active intervention of antipoverty workers helped limit the violence and property damage. (Both, courtesy of Providence Police Archive.)

Gang-related crime and vandalism also affected the city's public-housing developments. At the urging of tenants, the PPD in early 1971 established a 22-member force of community-protection officers (CPOs). The recruits underwent the same 17-week training regimen as police recruits and had admittedly dangerous assignments, but they were paid two-thirds the salary of regular officers, had no retirement benefits or overtime, and were unarmed. Attired in gray shirts with green pants, the first shift began work on the evening of June 16, 1971, at the Chad Brown and Roger Williams housing developments. Just after their arrival, they were immediately assaulted by roving gangs. A short time later, the CPOs were issued firearms. In 1978, the CPOs were reconstituted as the Housing Security Office. (Courtesy of the *Providence Journal*.)

The department's crossing guards pose outside city hall, sporting their new uniforms in the early 1970s. (Courtesy of Providence Police Archive.)

| Rudolph | James A. | Richard | James | John E. | Richard J. | Louis | Robert |
| SCIARRA | VESPIA | CALLEI | DUFFY | ROSSI | RICCI | MANOCCHIO | ALMONTE |

Tuesday, April 2, 1968

This 1968 lineup includes Louis "Baby Shanks" Manocchio (second from right), a Patriarca underboss who fled the country a year after this photograph was taken after having participated in the double murder of Rudolph Marfeo and Anthony Melei. He surrendered in 1979 and was given a 30-month sentence. Manocchio reportedly served as the head of the New England mob from 1996 to 2009. Also pictured is Rudolph "the Captain" Sciarra (far left), a mob enforcer. (Courtesy of Providence Police Archive.)

This is the interior of Coin-O-Matic Vending Machine Co. at 168 Atwells Avenue. It served as the mob headquarters for New England's crime boss Raymond Patriarca from the mid-1950s until his death on July 11, 1984. Known as "the Man," Patriarca was arrested dozens of times during his criminal career, and even while imprisoned for a double murder, he still found it easy to manage his criminal enterprise. (Courtesy of Providence Police Archive.)

As part of a campaign to create a new image for the PPD, Chief Walter McQueeney in 1972 replaced the standard blue uniform worn by officers for 107 years with a distinctive ensemble of tan pants and brown shirts, here being modeled by Sgt. Ted Collins. The cruiser to the right is also sporting new colors—brown and white. Uniforms were later adorned with a burnt-orange trim instituted by Col. Anthony J. Mancuso, who became chief of the department in May 1981. (Courtesy of the *Providence Journal*.)

The Traffic Division's motorcycle squad stands in front of PPD headquarters in 1961. The officer in the foreground is Lt. John J. Lucey, and in the background is Patrol Bureau commander George W. Wilding. In the distance is the old Hanley Brewery. (Courtesy of Providence Police Archive.)

Pictured here are officers at roll call in the central station. Donning their new brown-and-tan summer uniforms, these officers wear typical police equipment of the 1970s. Noticeably absent are the federal identification numbers (FID), which came into service in 1973. The FID numbers were required to be worn by all uniformed personnel of the PPD as a result of a federal court decree mandating greater accountability when dealing with the public. (Courtesy of the *Providence Journal*.)

This photograph of the covert task force of the 1970s includes four future police chiefs: Urbano "Barney" Prignano (front row, third from left), Richard Tamburini (front row, fourth from left), and Angelo Ricci (first row, right). Prignano and Ricci would become future police chiefs in Providence, while Tamburini later led the police force in Johnston. Robert Kells (back row, center) would become chief in Lincoln. Also known as the Tactical Squad, the group was organized to provide concentrated police scrutiny to high-crime areas of the city. Sporting plain clothes, the men carried out their assignments patrolling areas in used cars and trucks, sometimes wearing disguises. Occasionally, their aggressive tactics got the attention of the local press and the American Civil Liberties Union. (Courtesy of Providence Police Archive.)

In 1976, the 45th academy class included a record five females—from right to left, Dée Dee Nadrowski, Beth Comery, Nancy Kerrigan, Judy Mirando, and Jeanne Trafford. These recruits were for the first time included in all academy activities, including physical training and boxing. Upon graduation, they were designated patrolwomen and issued the same badge as men, but they were still required to be uniformed in skirts and white shirts, unlike their male counterparts, who wore brown-and-tan uniforms. For the first time, the female graduates were allowed to carry their weapons and gear on a duty belt. Skirts, however, soon proved impractical, especially when pursuing suspects over fences, and pants became standard for female officers as well. (Courtesy of Providence Police Archive.)

In 1977, the Providence Police Department recognized the need for a specialized unit to deal with ever-growing threats to public safety. A new Special Weapons and Tactics (SWAT) unit was formed, with training being carried out over a three-week period by members of the US Army Special Forces. This new PPD unit culminated its training in a display of readiness on May 13, 1977, with SWAT team member Ted Collins rappelling from the roof the Howard Building on Dorrance Street. (Courtesy of the *Providence Journal*.)

The great blizzard of 1978 began on the morning of February 6. Downtown workers, surprised by the growing intensity of the storm, jammed roads and highways, and by early afternoon, all ways out of the city were hopelessly clogged with cars and trucks. People simply abandoned their vehicles and sought shelter. Police headquarters at LaSalle Square became a makeshift hospital, and the bodies of several storm victims were placed in a temporary outdoor morgue at the rear of the building. Several resourceful policemen reportedly commandeered unattended four-wheel-drive military vehicles to aid in rescue or bring food to the hungry. The storm left the city under a blanket of three feet of snow. This photograph was taken on February 10. (Courtesy the *Providence Journal*.)

In the summer of 1979, Providence mayor Vincent A. Cianci Jr. proposed the reestablishment of a mounted patrol within the PPD. The following January, recruits were in training, and in March 1980, they made their first appearance on Providence streets. The unit was quartered at stables on Ernest Street. Pictured here atop their steeds are patrolmen Luis Del Rio (foreground), the department's first Hispanic officer, and Michael LaMarra. Del Rio would later rise to the rank of inspector as commanding officer of the Mounted Unit. (Courtesy of Providence Police Archive.)

Col. Walter E. Stone's career in local law enforcement spanned 58 years, and at the time of his death in 1997, he was considered by many to be "one of the nation's most respected police officers." Appointed to the department in October 1932, Stone quickly distinguished himself by foiling several armed robberies, culminating in the spectacular shoot-out at the Howard Johnson Restaurant in 1947. Promoted from sergeant to captain in a single move, he became one of the most decorated officers in the department's history. A strict disciplinarian operating with military-style efficiency, Stone was relentless in his campaign against organized crime. In 1959, he was named state police superintendent by Republican governor Chris DelSesto, but he was fired two years later by newly elected Democratic governor John A. Notte Jr. Stone returned to Providence briefly as police chief, but in 1963 was reappointed to the state police post by newly elected governor John H. Chafee. He remained at that post until retiring in 1990. (Courtesy of Providence Police Archive.)

Shown here on September 9, 1976, just after his swearing in as chief is Col. Robert E. Ricci, standing with three former chiefs of the Providence Police Department. From left to right are Cols. Walter T. McQueeney, Howard T. Franklin, Robert Ricci, and Walter E. Stone. (Courtesy of Providence Police Archive.)

Six

THE PROVIDENCE POLICE DEPARTMENT TODAY

1980–2014

As the Providence Police Department entered the 1980s, it benefitted from a new feeling of optimism sweeping the nation following an era of urban unrest and recession. During the early part of the decade, Providence mayor Vincent A. Cianci Jr. modernized the aging fleet of police vehicles, issued radios to each officer, and replaced revolvers with automatic pistols. The SWAT team was expanded and its firepower increased, and tactical training was intensified to include mutual exercises with other municipal SWAT teams. With the explosion of the crack cocaine epidemic in the late 1980s, the narcotics squad and patrol officers were tasked to the breaking point with an unprecedented spike in homicides, sudden deaths, drug activity, and housebreaks, resulting in a surge in calls for police services. During the 1990s, skillful union bargaining secured better health and vacation benefits as well as pay increases and a better pension package for FOP members. The union was also influential in securing passage of the Rhode Island Law Enforcement Officers Bill of Rights.

The year 1991 saw a return to the traditional blue uniform replacing the brown "sheriff's" uniform of the previous decade. New Mounted Command stables were built on a four-acre site in Roger Williams Park with funds provided by an Open Space and Recreation bond issue. Adoption of new technologies proceeded at an accelerating pace. Computers replaced the old Motorola radios in police vehicles, and advanced telecommunications equipment brought vast improvement to the police/fire communication department. Four officers were killed in the line of duty during this period, including Sgt. Steven Shaw—the first police officer killed by gunfire in over 50 years.

The Twin Towers attack in New York City on September 11, 2001, brought a wave of security challenges to the nation. The PPD responded by mandating homeland security training on weapons of mass destruction for all members, assessing structural vulnerabilities throughout the city, creating a harbor patrol, and participating in conferences on terrorism at the state and national levels. A new public-safety complex opened in 2002, replacing the outdated headquarters on Fountain Street. New leadership within the mayor's office and the police department placed a greater emphasis on "community policing," use of computer statistics (COMSTAT), and digitization of 40,000 fingerprints into the Automatic Fingerprint Identification System (AFIS) as a crime-fighting strategies.

With an active roster of 403 officers in early 2014, the PPD's strength is down more than 15 percent from its recent high of 487 officers in 1987. Severe recession and cutbacks in federal programs that funded community policing and violent-crime initiatives are partly responsible. A major initiative begun 10 years ago that resulted in the creation of nine neighborhood-based police districts was recently cut to seven. Despite this loss of personnel, however, the crime rate has remained steady and, although taxed to the limit, the men and women of the department responded to more than 123,000 calls for service in 2013. A new police academy scheduled for spring 2014 will bring a fresh crop of recruits to supplement the PPD's ranks and help the department carry out its 150-year mission to keep Providence and its citizens safe.

In July 1981, the city of Providence was embroiled in a labor dispute sparked by a fiscal crisis that led to a cut in overtime pay for the city's garbage collectors. Violent threats were made when the mayor replaced striking sanitation workers and brought in a private company to collect garbage. Trucks had to be hidden at secret rendezvous points to prevent vandalism, and the mayor himself received death threats, prompting 24-hour police protection. Here, Mayor Cianci instructs shotgun-toting patrolman Robert Chin as he climbs aboard a garbage truck for guard duty. (Courtesy of the *Providence Journal*.)

Patrolmen Frank Moody (left) and Clarence Gough, having apprehended a suspect on Weybosset Street, appear as if they may be answering to a higher calling. (Courtesy of Clarence Gough.)

By the 1980s, police communication had come a long way from the days of the desktop transmitter. Here, operators in the control center field telephone calls for service and write the required information on a card. This card was then placed on a conveyor belt and sent up to the dispatcher. Should the call be of an urgent nature, the operator would yell out to the dispatcher, "I have an emergency call," and that call would take precedence over less-urgent calls. (Courtesy of Providence Police Archive.)

The police department received a new fleet of vehicles in 1982. Here, Patrolman Frank Zienowicz shows off the new police cars. These new Ford Fairmonts were quite unpopular with the officers as they were very compact and left little room for the taller individuals. (Courtesy of the *Providence Journal*.)

In a 6-second span, a criminal dies and his hostage survives

Story by Christopher Scanlan with reports from Paul Duggan, Ira Chinoy, Doane Hulick, Ward Pimley, Dave Crombie and S. Robert Chiappinelli.

PROVIDENCE — John A. Hicks held Ptlm. Osvaldo Castillo in a captor's embrace, his arm coiled around the patrolman's throat, the

Wounded policeman helps
Hispanics Page C1

barrel of a gun pressed into the soft flesh of his neck.

It was shortly after 9 a.m. yesterday. On a quiet residential street, a bank robbery gone sour had become a matter of life or death for two men: a desperate parolee with a record of bank robbery and kidnapping, and a young Hispanic patrolman making a name for himself in one of the toughest beats in the city.

"If I die," Hicks told the police who surrounded him and Patrolman Castillo, "he's going to die."

★ ★ ★

THE FLEET National Bank's Washington Park branch at 1473 Broad St. had just opened for business. There were four customers and 12 employees inside when John Hicks and another man pushed open the glass doors and walked inside. Hicks headed for the teller on the far right. The other man stood by the door. He held a sawed-off shotgun.

Hicks pointed a pistol at the teller, held out a black bag and told her to fill it. But the woman was too frightened to move. Hicks vaulted the counter and grabbed the money, leaving behind packets of cash rigged with red dye and an explosive device. He moved to the next teller and emptied her drawer. His accomplice left the door and ordered another teller to give him the contents of her drawer.

Carrying about $9,000, the robbers headed for the door, turned

After a 1982 bank robbery in the Washington Park section of the city, police were called to search for the suspects. Responding to the call for assistance was Patrolman Osvaldo Castillo, who was taken hostage by one of the robbers at gunpoint. During the course of this incident and an ensuing gun battle, Castillo was wounded but survived. The bank robber was not so lucky. (Courtesy of the *Providence Journal*.)

The Providence Police Special Response Unit participated in many training exercises. In this 1987 photograph, Providence and Warwick police participate in a joint sniper-training exercise. Pictured here in the center is instructor Carlos Hathcock, whose reputation was legendary as a sniper in the Vietnam War. (Courtesy of Providence Police Archive.)

On July 28, 1988, during a raid on a notorious drug gang in the Hartford Park development, Sgt. Thomas Oates (kneeling, right), author George Pearson (kneeling, left), and FBI agent James Burkett are seen here apprehending a suspect. A large amount of weapons and drugs were also seized as part of this incident. (Courtesy of the *Providence Journal*.)

Mayor Joseph R. Paolino Jr. (left) is pictured here with John J. Partington during his swearing-in ceremony as commissioner of public safety on December 21, 1989. Partington was widely known within the law-enforcement community as a highly regarded US marshal and is credited with helping create the Federal Witness Protection Program. In 1990, Commissioner Partington replaced the brown-and-tan police uniforms with traditional blue. (Courtesy of Providence City Archives.)

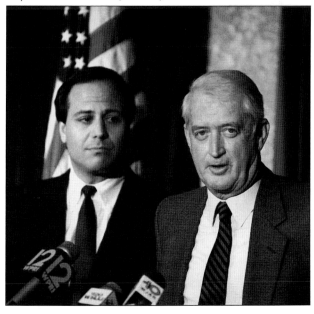

Patrolman Allen Spiver is seen here modeling the new blue uniform. In the background is the newly designed white police vehicle with the blue stripe. (Courtesy of Providence Police Archive.)

In 1991, a new bicycle unit was formed as part of the department's efforts to enhance community policing. Here, members of this new unit stand in Kennedy Plaza. (Courtesy of Providence Police Archive.)

In 1992, members of the Special Response Unit received commendations from the police department for a hostage incident on Babcock Street. Here, Patrolman Steven T. Shaw receives his commendation from Col. Bernard E. Gannon as Maj. William V. Devine looks on. Patrolman Shaw would be killed in the line of duty in February 1994. (Courtesy of Providence Police Archive.)

Here, members of the day Traffic Bureau stand in ranks at the dedication of a new fleet of Traffic Bureau vehicles in 1994. Future chief Richard T. Sullivan (front row, second from right) is pictured next to Col. Bernard E. Gannon (front row, far right). (Courtesy of Taft Manzotti.)

In 1994, police department representatives attended the National Law Enforcement Officers Memorial in Washington, DC, in memory of Patrolman Steven Shaw. Here, the executive board of the Providence Police Lodge 3, Fraternal Order of Police, stands on the National Mall in front of the Washington Monument. Pictured, from left to right, are Patrolman Robert Clements, Det. Jack Murray, retired officer Ray Pezzullo, Det. Dan Driscoll, FOP president Patrolman Mike Marcoccio, and FOP vice president Sgt. Hugh Clements. (Courtesy of Providence Police Archive.)

Cornel Young was promoted to major in 1995, becoming the first African American to achieve that rank. Several years later, Major Young's son Patrolman Cornel Young Jr. was tragically killed in the line of duty. (Courtesy of Providence Police Archive.)

Mayor Vincent Cianci leads a contingent of police in the 2000 Bristol Fourth of July parade. Among the marchers are Col. Bernard Gannon, Maj. Gerald Aubin, Maj. Stephen McCartney (later to become chief of the Warwick Police Department), and Maj. Richard T. Sullivan (future chief of the Providence Police Department). (Courtesy of Providence Police Archive.)

The police department has been patrolling the city's housing developments since the Providence Housing Authority (PHA) opened its doors to tenants at the outset of World War II. In the early 1970s, the department assigned a specialized unit to ensure order at the housing developments. Patrolmen Jack Costa (left) and Paul "Porky" O'Rourke have spent their entire police careers serving the PHA and its residents. They are well respected by both the residents and the entire community. (Courtesy of Jack Costa.)

Shortly after the tragic events in New York City on September 11, 2001, members of the Providence Police Department were dispatched to assist the New York Police Department in its efforts to restore order and provide relief to its exhausted officers. Pictured here are members of the Providence Police Department in front of the Midtown North Precinct in Manhattan. (Courtesy of Ed Malloy.)

In 2002, the 60-year-old central police and fire headquarters at 209 Fountain Street was replaced with an impressive new 130,000-square-foot facility constructed on a rise of land overlooking Interstate 95. Built at an estimated cost of nearly $50 million, the building features a distinctive multistory glass atrium, enlarged office space for police and fire personnel, a fitness center, and quarters for the municipal and housing courts. One major plus is an adjacent parking garage, an amenity sorely lacking in the old headquarters, which was subsequently demolished and the site of which currently being used as a parking lot. (Courtesy of Providence Police Archive.)

James Shea was a Providence police officer for 28 years, retiring in 1953. He was interviewed by Det. George Pearson in 2001 at the age of 100 and clearly remembered his days as member of the Flying Squadron during the Prohibition era when Sergeant Flynn and Patrolman O'Brien were killed. Officer Shea passed away at age 105 in 2006. (Courtesy of Providence Police Archive and David Shea.)

Dean Esserman was sworn in as Providence Police Chief on January 10, 2003. A graduate of Dartmouth College and the New York University Law School, Esserman had served as a Special US Attorney in New York and as chief of the New Haven and Stamford, Connecticut, police departments before arriving in Providence. A strong proponent of community policing, Esserman also implemented PROVSTAT, a computer-based program to analyze, track, and predict crime trends, based on New York's successful COMSTAT model. (Courtesy of Providence Police Archive.)

With the ever-growing terrorist threats throughout the world, the Providence Police Department responded by expanding its Bomb Unit. Here, Sgt. Robert Boehm helps a member of the unit get into his bomb suit. (Courtesy of Providence Police Archive.)

The Special Response Unit has trained in the newest techniques and is outfitted with the latest equipment. (Courtesy of Providence Police Archive.)

Operating in conjunction with Homeland Security, the Harbor Unit, boasting a new, well-equipped SAFE patrol boat, maintains a watchful eye on the Providence waterfront and shipping lanes along the Providence River. (Courtesy of Providence Police Archive.)

Col. Hugh T. Clements is seen here at the scene of a police-vehicle accident that took the life of officer Maxwell R. Dorley. Officer Dorley was killed on April 19, 2012, while en route to assist another officer who had called for urgent assistance. (Courtesy of the *Providence Journal*.)

During the past 20 years, four Providence police officers have been killed in the line of duty—Sgt. Stephen M. Shaw, Sgt. Cornel Young Jr., Sgt. James L. Allen, and Sgt. Maxwell R. Dorley. (Courtesy of Maj. Thomas Verdi, PPD.)

The Providence Police Department has trained its recruits through the Providence Police Training Academy since 1946. Although the department has trained its officers in police tactics since 1864, an organized, official training academy was not established until 1946. The Providence Police Training Academy is Rhode Island POST–certified (Police Officers Commission on Standards & Training) and is the only city-run academy in the state. Shown is the latest graduating academy recruit class in 2010 along with instructors (seated). (Courtesy of Maj. Thomas Verdi, PPD.)

Col. Hugh T. Clements stands surrounded by the PPD command staff. Shown are, from left to right, Maj. Francisco Colon, Comdr. Thomas Oates, Colonel Clements, Maj. Thomas Verdi, and Maj. David Lapatin. (Courtesy of officer Ron Pino, PPD, January 2014.)

Police communication has come a long way during the past century. Here, Cory Fusco works at PPD's state-of-the-art communications center, fielding calls for service and dispatch. Last year, the center received more than 123,000 calls for service. (Courtesy of officer Ron Pino, PPD.)

The Providence Police Pipes and Drums are shown here during the St. Patrick's Day parade in Newport, Rhode Island. This 18-member pipe band is the only police department pipe band in the state. (Courtesy of PPD Pipes and Drums.)

Shown here are the badges of the Providence Police Department. From left to right, they were issued in (top row) 1845, 1864, and 1881; (bottom row) 1948, and 1994. (Courtesy of Providence Police Archive.)

Known affectionately as "The Dancing Cop," officer Tony Lepore began directing downtown traffic in 1984 and recalls that out of boredom he started using dance moves and acrobatic gyrations in an effort to move traffic along. Although he retired in 1988, Lepore's growing popularity prompted local officials in 1992 to bring him back annually for encore performances to the delight of December holiday shoppers making their way along busy Dorrance Street. (Courtesy of Tony Lepore.)

Providence Police Officers Killed in Action

Policeman William T. Pullen	(May 18, 1852)
Patrolman John F. Brennan	(April 2, 1911)
Patrolman James P. Cavanaugh	(Decemeber 26, 1916)
Sergeant William A. Flynn	(February 12, 1928)
Patrolman James H. O'Brien	(Febrary 12, 1928)
Patrolman Thomas A. Mulvey	(September 19, 1931)
Sergeant Steven M. Shaw	(February 3, 1994)
Sergeant Cornel Young, Jr.	(January 28, 2000)
Detective Sergeant James Allen	(April 17, 2005)
Sergeant Maxwell R. Dorley	(April 19, 2012)

During the past 162 years, ten Providence police officers have given their lives in the line of duty. (Courtesy of Providence Police Archive.)

127

DISCOVER THOUSANDS OF LOCAL HISTORY BOOKS
FEATURING MILLIONS OF VINTAGE IMAGES

Arcadia Publishing, the leading local history publisher in the United States, is committed to making history accessible and meaningful through publishing books that celebrate and preserve the heritage of America's people and places.

Find more books like this at
www.arcadiapublishing.com

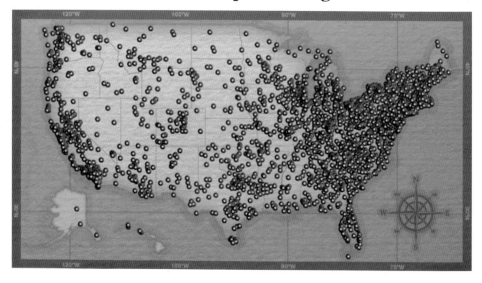

Search for your hometown history, your old stomping grounds, and even your favorite sports team.